D0437728

The Heart of Godly Leadership

The Heart of Godly Leadership

Hudson T. Armerding

CROSSWAY BOOKS • WHEATON, ILLINOIS
A DIVISION OF GOOD NEWS PUBLISHERS

Library of Congress Cataloging-in-Publication Data
Armerding, Hudson T.
    The heart of godly leadership / Hudson T. Armerding.
        p.   cm.
    Includes bibliographical references and index.
    1. Christian leadership.   I. Title.
BV652.A73 1992   253—dc20   92-6453
ISBN 0-89107-675-1

00		99		98		97		96		95		94		93		92
15	14	13	12	11	10	9	8	7	6	5	4	3	2	1

CONTENTS

INTRODUCTION

Leadership is an absorbing, challenging, and sometimes threatening experience. A college president once compared it to a boy walking on top of a picket fence. He finds the experience exhilarating, but one misstep will put him in danger of being impaled. It is this combination of challenge and concern that is realistically recognized by the conscientious leader, particularly when God's calling to the position is a major factor in the acceptance of this assignment.

Yet not all in the Christian community perceive the administrative task in this light. By contrast, some consider its importance significantly less than that of the minister, missionary, or evangelist. Such an assessment fails to take into account the many-faceted aspects of God's work in the world, with each component essential to the success of the entire enterprise.

What those in administrative work need, however, is more than recognition. They deserve guidance and support. Recognizing this, mature leaders often express the wish that those who are destined to follow them might profit from their experiences and insights.

This is my sentiment as well. After a lifetime in various executive positions, I have come to understand the remarkable way in which the truths of the Bible are pertinent to the leadership role. These delineate a proven standard of excellence for the guidance of the one seeking God's best in fulfilling the calling to lead.

The conclusions I have reached over the years helped shape the contents of this book. But the initial manuscript would never have been written without the encouragement and practical implementation provided by Lt. Col. Arnold Sanderlin, USA (Ret.) of the Officers Christian Fellowship staff. He persuasively conveyed his vision for a work of this kind and helped create a climate of acceptance for it. Then, when a revision was contemplated, I found in Mrs. Diana Weistart of Phoenix a renewal of the vision combined with the skills necessary to incorporate other ministry emphases of mine into a new manuscript. In addition, her husband Barth and their daughter Mara furnished the technical support required to produce a text that could be distributed for critical appraisal. This evaluation was gladly given by Professor Paul Eymann and others in Phoenix and by Dr. J. Robertson McQuilkin, now chancellor of Columbia Bible College and Seminary where he gave distinguished presidential leadership for twenty-two years. I greatly appreciated his thoughtful and incisive critique and his charity in those few instances when I was disposed to maintain an opinion different from his.

William J. Bonner, president of the Quarryville Presbyterian Retirement Community, where I am now employed, has been gracious in providing a quiet and tasteful setting for my work, efficient secretarial support, and sufficient time for reflective thinking about the strategic role of Christian leadership.

Throughout the many months dedicated to the writing and rewriting of the manuscript I have had the prayer support and encouragement of the one who has stood with me during the long and sometimes stressful years of my leadership pilgrimage—my wife, Miriam. With growing appreciation I dedicate this volume to her.

Hudson Taylor Armerding
Quarryville, Pennsylvania
February 20, 1992

1

A Pause for Perspective

L eadership is a calling which is exacting both in its demands on the leader and on those who attempt to fulfill the leader's expectations.

Frustration results when a leader is perceived as an intruder. Such was the case in an organization where the leader assigned a certain task to a subordinate and then kept telling him in detail how to do it. Finally, in exasperation, the subordinate handed back the assignment and told his superior he might as well do it himself.

This all too common occurrence makes God's willingness to delegate responsibilities to His creatures so very remarkable. The first dramatic evidence of such delegation was at the creation when God gave to human beings the oversight over all that He had made. We call this "the creation mandate." From this foundational responsibility a pattern was set for the institutions that God ordained for the welfare of the human community. Adam and Eve were to rule over the creation and take care of it (Genesis 1:26, 28; 2:15), but were at one and the same time the rulers and the ruled, being subordinate to God and accountable to Him for their stewardship.

The structures of the family, the community of faith, human government, and economic institutions were all to have this same dual character of leading and following, shepherding and submitting, ruling and being ruled, directing and being directed. This awareness of interdependence should promote in the life of the leader an appropriate humility, resulting not in excessive self-abnegation but instead in a refreshing recognition of the significance of a role that is not dependent simply on status but on empowering by God.

Leadership within the Christian community, then, not only applies to interaction between those directing and those being directed, but also reflects the divine-human relationship. This relationship is essential to the calling, the equipping, and the shaping of the leader. Furthermore, the constructive results of this process provide structure and direction in the practice of Christian leadership.

Encouragement Through Example

One of the most effective ways in which God illuminates His Biblical teaching about leadership is through the example set by those who have perceptively responded to precept and experience under the good hand of God. This tangible demonstration saves the abstract and the propositional from irrelevancy and generates both understanding and hope. In other words, the task is both meaningful and possible and is of ultimate significance as well as immediate pertinence.

Vitality Generated by Interdependence

The Biblical view of leadership also is characterized by coherence and intimate relationship. To illustrate this, our Lord Jesus Christ used a powerful and meaningful metaphor, telling His disciples He was the Vine and they were the branches. As branches they were dependent upon Him, the Vine, for their vitality. Similarly, an organization receives its vision, inspiration, and intellectual and emotional nurturing from its leadership.

Also significant is the fact that the Vine "needs" the branches, we might say, to accomplish its reason for being. For inscrutable purposes, our Lord has chosen to have His followers bear the fruit He wills to produce.

Seasoned executives are aware that the vine-and-branches analogy is true of their organization. The leaders provide the necessary oversight, direction, and inspiration, but it is their colleagues and subordinates who actually get the specific tasks done. Only in this way is "much fruit" produced. Perhaps it is appropriate to suggest that there is a mutual set of obligations and responsibilities in the interaction between leader and follower that brings about the desired outcome. We recognize that in the divine-human relationship it is more a matter of God's selecting this way to work out the purposes He has ordained rather than any dependency on His part that requires our contribution to the cause. But this does not invalidate the pertinence of the principle as it is applied in such structures of human society as the home, the church, the state, or the economic order.

Particularly in the functioning of the church is the analogy of the body used appropriately to highlight the interdependency of each part (1 Corinthians 12). This chapter of Scripture eloquently and forcefully underscores the leader's need for followers (e.g., the eye and the hand, the head and the foot) and the importance of the subordinates (e.g., the foot, the ear) in the efficient functioning of the body. No part should conclude that because it is not more significant, visible or attractive, it is therefore not vital to the body. I submit that such a perspective is essential to both leaders and followers, managers and subordinates, pastors and people.

Intimacy and Outreach

Another Biblical principle drawn from the pattern set by God Himself is the balance between intimacy and outreach. In viewing God's care for His own as that of Father to children, there is a necessary inference that within the Christian community there should be nurturing and protection and opportunities for very personal and private interchange.

Unfortunately this beautiful, winsome model is too often perceived as the only one to be followed, thus resulting in misguided introspection on the part of both the leader and those who follow his direction. Admittedly, in this structure one finds comfort and security, but one also experiences isolation and withdrawal. While not in any way diminishing the importance of caring leadership in a closely knit community of faith, I am persuaded that fellowship, nurture, and worship are only part of that which Christian leadership should cultivate. We must also recognize and emphasize following our Lord's example in His coming into the world, His seeking the lost, His being the light of the world, His confronting the forces of evil, His bearing witness to truth in the marketplace. Sadly, too often Christian leadership has concentrated on the provincial or the functional without summoning their associates to penetrate the social, political, and economic realms as the salt of the earth and the light of the world.

One reason for the reluctance to undertake such a daunting task is this: Throughout redemptive history God's people have been a minority—sometimes tolerated, often ignored, on occasion forcefully confronted and persecuted. This we will endure only through Jesus Christ, for by nature human beings desire to be accepted and appreciated. Even radicals who seem to thrive on polarization and confrontation seek for association and acceptance in cults, gangs, societies, or parties.

In light of these considerations, the Christian leader is faced with a formidable challenge. The distinctiveness of the Christian cause must be maintained or the watching world has no viable alternative to consider. Yet that very distinctiveness, to be authentic, prompts reaction and resistance, for it is perceived as an uncomfortable intrusion into a social structure which has concluded that God is irrelevant to its manner of life.

Subtle Threats to Effective Leadership

Historically a minority which takes the offensive also has had to face the reality of a counter-penetration that often succeeds by enticement rather than aggression. Consider the allurements of conspicuous consumption and self-gratification that have had a demonstrably powerful appeal within the evangelical world. The mournful record testifies to the triumph of this approach, particularly when the leadership is the first to capitulate.

One of the most salutary lessons I have learned through both observation and participation is the necessity of settled conviction and of resoluteness of purpose balanced by a perspective that is able to sort out the essential from the incidental, the immutable from the negotiable. Leading a minority community thus requires the insight and skill needed to maintain the coherence and integrity of the fellowship of God's people and at the same time succeed in being in the world but not of it. As we shall see, Biblical examples will illuminate this issue both by documented failure and by celebrated triumph. The realism of Scripture both warns and inspires. This is why I believe an understanding of Biblical revelation is essential to the perspective of the Christian leader.

Detachment Necessary to Perspective

A key element of a balanced perspective involves dealing realistically with the isolation or detachment leaders experience by virtue of their office. In my experience, both in the military and in academic administration, there was an invisible and yet very tangible separation that made previous close associations no longer an option. I think this degree of detachment is a requirement for objectivity and for the elimination of partisanship. But it also can result in a loneliness that is exacerbated by unpopular decisions even when those decisions are based upon principle rather than prejudice or provincialism.

Discipline Crucial to Leadership

The successful leader must also cultivate one of the major characteristics of maturity: the ability to defer gratification. Learning not to cater to oneself is no simple task. Leadership is usually envisioned as a companion of privilege and power. It takes an uncommon degree of discipline to avoid using these accoutrements to manipulate or exploit the dependent or the unwary.

Generally speaking, being caught up in a cause helps a leader escape distractions and at the same time feel secure in warm and caring service to subordinates or supporters. And the satisfaction generated by accomplishment is recompense enough and is far less ephemeral than the fickle applause of those captivated by dramatic exhibitionism rather than by consistent devotion.

Evidence of Supernatural Preparation

How a leader develops disciplined qualities is sometimes perceived as strictly a matter of natural talent, experience, and a liberal admixture of what our world would call good fortune—the leader was fortunate enough to be at the right place at the right time. I concur that there are indeed strategic occasions which seem to cry out for decisive initiative at the right moment. I am also convinced that the structuring of events comes by divine appointment and is accompanied by supernatural preparation. We shall consider Biblical instances of this, the most celebrated being the incarnation of our Lord Himself in what the Scriptures call "the fullness of time" (cf., for example, Galatians 4:4 and similar passages). Divine appointment is clear here, though He was also obviously superbly prepared for His earthly ministry, both before His incarnation and after it, and has shown the results of this in His promised presence with His followers of all ages, including ours. Being fully man as well as fully God, He learned obedience by what He suffered, and in the process achieved a completeness that was vital to His saving work (Hebrews 5:8, 9). Through the inscrutable workings of our sovereign God we too are both gifted and fashioned by divine provision and process and are steadied in our growing spirituality by fixing our eyes on Jesus and having His mind in us.

Timing One's Retirement

In a far more mundane way we leaders can furnish to our followers both an exhibition of godly ministry and needed inspiration for their own pilgrimage toward maturity and usefulness. I have learned that we are most effective when our portrayal incorporates testing as well as triumph, inspiring initiatives and equally inspiring endings in our careers. The checkered record of Christian leadership validates the observation that few finish well. Alacrity in response to opportunity is usually much more frequent than decisiveness in passing the torch. As we shall see in Chapter 16, the decision to withdraw or retire can be the most formidable challenge a leader faces. And I suggest that it is at this point the measure of a leader is taken. I am not thinking of sentimental reviews of the faded glories of the past. To be sure, retrospect is important in the growing awareness of God's providence, but it should not degenerate into a romanticism more fanciful than actual. I am thinking of much more than that.

Is Leadership Worth It All?

For some the questions may well be: Why endure the rigors, the salutary but perhaps painful shapings, the inevitable misunderstandings, the ephemeral or quixotic acceptances, the shallow and often insincere endorsements, the adversarial posturings of those whose experience is devoid of major responsibility or accountability? In the long span of history, honor and recognition are transitory indeed, as a visit to the site of any ancient civilization will attest. Why give your life to what in time will be a fragmented statue or a crumbled inscription?

The answer to this question lies in the eternity of God—in His immutable purposes, in His inexorable justice, in His incomprehensible mercy. While refusing to share His glory with another, He promises enduring rewards and recognition that eclipse even the most sustained admiration of a grateful society for its durable heroes. But recognition—ultimate if not immediate—should not be our primary motivation. Instead, our response to God's calling us to lead is rooted in our awareness that we belong to Him, the Almighty God and the Everlasting Father, not only as His creatures but also as His by redemption. We must follow and obey Him.

Our response, then, ought to incorporate both reverence and commitment—worship that is expressed in sacrifice—love and gratitude that spring gladly from awakened hearts and minds, based on the perception of liberated spirits that places the temporal and the eternal in proper juxtaposition.

All this is not drawn from our limited, fallible human resources but is the splendid product of divine enabling. I submit that responding to the call to lead, as we incorporate this perspective, makes any alternative unthinkable. What in all the world could transcend the urgency and yet the sublimity of doing the will of God? Thus with Augustine we pray, "Give what Thou commandest, and then command what Thou wilt."

How wonderful it is that God elicits our response to His invitation to do His will rather than consigning us to a wholly passive state in which we serve Him puppetlike—automatons rather than participants. Surely this, too, is all of grace. It is personal rather than mechanical. For me the difference is immense, incalculable, and not fully comprehensible—and yet tangible and real. Awareness results in reverence, response, resolve. With our Savior we can say, "I delight to do Your will, O My God." Thus we may respond to the question, Why be a leader? with another: Why not?

This book has been written for those who have posed the second question.

2

The Refiner's Fire

We will continue our discussion of Christian leadership by considering generally what the Scriptures have to say about trials which come to those God has called to lead.

"Blessed are those who are persecuted because of righteousness, for theirs is the kingdom of heaven. Blessed are you when people insult you, persecute you and falsely say all kinds of evil against you because of me. Rejoice and be glad, because great is your reward in heaven, for in the same way they persecuted the prophets who were before you." (Matthew 5:10-12)

Individuals new to leadership may be taken off guard by troubles that seem to emerge almost immediately. Consider one of the questions frequently asked in Christian circles: "Why me, Lord?" This question is not absent from the vocabulary of those in positions of responsibility. Besides recognizing the minority status and interdependence of the Christian community, the leader must accept the inevitability of trials and testings as a critical component of the refining process. The Lord Jesus said His people would experience such difficulties in the world. Both observation and experience now and in history provide ample documentation of the fulfillment of this prediction.

Gaining by Losing

It is one thing to endure the inevitability of trouble and quite another to deal with it constructively. The Apostle Paul addressed this dilemma when he declared, "we also rejoice in our sufferings" (Romans 5:3). As we have seen, the same emphasis appears in the Sermon on the Mount, in which our Lord taught that we are "blessed" when we are persecuted. This principle is consistent with other Scriptures, such as our Lord's declaration, "For whoever wants to save his life will lose it, but whoever loses his life for me and for the gospel will save it" (Mark 8:35).

An assertion that one can gain by losing appears absurd to the non-Christian. And when we tell unbelievers about the blessing promised those who are persecuted, they may conclude that we are psychologically abnormal. These Biblical injunctions are addressed exclusively to the redeemed community who are informed by the Holy Spirit and are thus able to accept a Biblical insight that transcends purely human speculations.

The Lord Jesus speaks to believers, therefore, when He declares, "Blessed are you when people insult you, persecute you and falsely say all kinds of evil against you because of me." Certain illustrations help us to understand what our Savior had in mind when He made this statement. Consider one from our Lord's own experience as recorded in Matthew 27:39-44. This passage tells us that those who passed by hurled insults at Him, and the religious leaders mocked Him. Even the robbers crucified with Him heaped insults on Him. All the while the Lord Jesus remained stretched upon the cross. Because of the sovereign will of God, He could not come down; He had to bear His suffering. He did not even respond when His revilers took specific statements and twisted them out of context to concoct their accusations. He is our example!

Categories of Trouble

Hence, *being insulted* comprises one kind of treatment a Christian can expect. We will experience occasions when we will be unable to defend ourselves because of our commitment to the purposes of God; obedience to His commands will sometimes prevent us from responding. As was true of our Lord, our statements made in integrity will be distorted and turned back against us—often without opportunity for rebuttal.

In addition to the description of insults, Scripture is replete with illustrations of *persecution*. A particularly focused one is found in Philippians 3. The Apostle Paul described his treatment of the church before he became a believer in this way: "as for zeal, persecuting the church" (v. 6). An elaboration can be found in the book of Acts. The last part of chapter 7 reports Paul's participation in the stoning of Stephen. The next two chapters recount Paul's entering the houses of Christians and ensuring that believers were put into prison; then he breathed out murderous threats on his way to Damascus. What the Apostle Paul inflicted upon the church before he became a Christian gives us a Scriptural illustration of some aspects of persecution: invasion of privacy, removal of rights, denial of a fair trial.

The third category of trouble involves *having all kinds of evil spoken against us falsely*, for Jesus' sake. The experience of our Lord Jesus Christ as recorded in Matthew 26:57-68 illustrates this. The religious leaders diligently sought false witnesses against Jesus and finally found two who would do their bidding. Hence, the high priest's interrogation and condemnation of our Savior was based on a misrepresentation of the evidence.

I suspect that after the disciples had seen the events leading up to the crucifixion, our Lord's statement about "blessing" during trouble must have come back to them with great force—especially to Peter, who had personally observed what took place. Therefore, it would not have been difficult for the disciples to conclude that false accusers would be hired to discredit *their* testimony, even as had been done against their Savior.

Who Are the Persecutors?

In light of the Scripture that declares we are "blessed" when people insult and persecute us, we should ask these questions: Who are the persecutors, and who are the persecuted? Are any of us among the persecuted?

The original language provided no specific word in this text for people who persecute believers, and so the translators simply supplied the term that was implied. Certainly people do the actual persecuting, reviling, and evil speaking. But I believe they are acting on behalf of a being who has set himself in opposition to the Lord and therefore to the Lord's people. That evil being is Satan.

You see an instance of Satan's buffeting in the book of Job. When the various beings came to present themselves before the Lord, Satan also came. The Lord asked him if he had considered Job. Satan had indeed done so, but he knew the Lord was protecting His servant. Satan then received permission to afflict Job but was to spare his life. Satan did not directly inflict the catastrophes but used the weather, the Sabeans, and the Chaldeans to do so.

Opposition also comes through other spiritual adversaries. Daniel, for example, had prayed but had received no answer (Daniel 10:12, 13). When an angel finally came, he told Daniel that the prince of the kingdom of Persia had withstood him for twenty-one days. Who was this prince? I think he was one of Satan's emissaries who was doing battle with God's messenger in the spiritual realm. Recall also that Paul in Ephesians 6 tells us that our warfare is with spiritual forces of evil (v. 12).

I suggest, therefore, that when the insulting and the persecution and the false statements come, it is Satan who is actually directing this onslaught against the Christian, and he is using his children and various devices in an attempt to achieve his purposes. Further insights may be gained from the incident when our Lord Jesus was confronted by those who challenged His statements. He said they were doing the deeds of their father, the Devil (John 8:44). Thus an integral relationship exists between Satan and those who follow his direction in opposing the Lord and His people.

Such opposition makes our Lord's words—"for my sake," "for me," "because of me," and so on—so meaningful. We are not important in Satan's estimation for our own sakes. His only reason for attacking us is that we bear the name of Christ. Thus we are his enemies.

Who Are the Persecuted?

This question highlights an important issue: does our Savior's statement apply to all believers? Certainly some Christians have suffered persecution. Others have not had the same intensity of experience.

I recall my first night in the military. When I knelt by my bunk to pray, other men walked by and kicked my feet and my legs. Even so, I was not really insulted. There was some ridicule, but nothing akin to what happened to our Savior. Furthermore, I have never had the experience of having my home entered, nor of being arrested and put in jail for my faith. Nor have I stood trial and had false witnesses testify against me to convict me.

What, then, should we conclude? Does the Savior's statement apply only to a segment of Christians at particular times such as the Inquisition, or to locations such as Mainland China or North Korea? I do not believe so. When we think of persecution, we tend to consider it to be visible, physical, and material. This is understandable, for the Bible documents such persecution. The Lord Jesus physically suffered upon a literal cross. The people who accused Him in fact shouted out their accusations and reproaches. The early Christians were actually taken from their homes and imprisoned. But are these the only ways in which Christians have been persecuted? Our experience testifies to the contrary.

I know of a gifted man who was called of God to a creative and difficult ministry. His church intersected two different communities— one impoverished, the other countercultural and having blatantly sinful practices. This man directed his ministry for the Lord toward both of these neighborhoods.

After a period of years, a friend learned of the man's strong inclination to leave the ministry. When asked why, the man told his friend about being overwhelmed by futility and despair and feeling driven to consider some other calling.

I recognize that emotional depression increasingly afflicts many in our country, often at a time in life that brings major emotional upheavals. But this man's experiences did not fit into this category.

Following a discussion of the minister's feelings, his friend asked God to rebuke the enemy so he would not overwhelm this gifted and sensitive servant of the Lord. While not outward or physical, the persecution proved to be formidable and required divine deliverance.

I faced a similar crisis in my spirit during a brief study leave on a ranch in West Texas. Living alone in the old ranch house, I would work on manuscripts in the mornings and then go out in the afternoon to do ranching. Most of the time I prepared my own meals. After lunch one noon I was washing the dishes. All during the forenoon a disturbing memory had kept coming to my attention—an act of disobedience years before that I had confessed and by grace had put away. Yet repeatedly that morning the recollection kept coming back, constant accusations that would not cease.

But as I bent over the dishes, suddenly this word came just as clearly as if someone were in the room: "If we walk in the light, as he is in the light, we have fellowship one with another, and the blood of Jesus Christ his Son cleanseth us from all sin" (1 John 1:7, KJV).

I knew that a more accurate translation would read, ". . . *continues* to cleanse us from all sin*." Immediately tears mingled with the dishwater because the Lord Jesus in mercy and through the Holy Spirit had reminded me of the unchanging truth of His word of forgiveness on the basis of His atoning sacrifice. Thus God overcame the persecution of Satan that was calculated to imprison me in guilt and to challenge the deliverance wrought by the Lord.

Such persecution has a dreadful reality to it. I believe furthermore that the more strategic your position as a Christian leader, the more you will face this kind of persecution. As I have come to know Christians in responsible positions, I have learned of similar experiences they have undergone. So the fact that people do not literally shout at us or drag us off to prison or bring false witness against us in a court of law does not mean that the enemy is not doing exactly what the Lord Jesus said he would do against the Christian. Christ's words in John 16:33 remain true: "In this world you will have trouble." But He went on, "But take heart! I have overcome the world." Thankfully, in Christ we overcome the enemy.

Suffering for Christ's Sake

Faced with the reality and the inevitability of persecution, how can we understand the Lord's promise, "blessed are you"? It would be incomplete to say, "Blessed are you when people insult you, persecute you and falsely say all kinds of evil against you" and stop there. Some might use this as a rationalization to justify their avoidance of responsibility for their own faults and sins. In such cases we cannot consider ourselves blessed, for we must take into account the Apostle Peter's statement that if we suffer it should not be as evildoers (1 Peter 3:17). Let us ask ourselves frankly whether or not it is for Jesus' sake or for our own wrongdoing that we are being persecuted.

If we indeed suffer for Christ's sake, then what our Savior said provides both *prospect* and *retrospect*, to make our *perspective* complete. Both prospect and retrospect are found in the words, "great is your reward in heaven, for in the same way they persecuted the prophets who were before you" (Matthew 5:12).

Retrospect enables us to reflect upon the experiences of the prophets of old, many of whom were persecuted for their faith.

Within the context of Christian discipleship, we should consider their example and particularly that of our Savior because the Christian, as a redeemed person, has the capacity to respond to creative examples. The Apostle Peter put it this way: "Christ suffered for you, leaving you an example, that you should follow in his steps . . ." (1 Peter 2:21). The Christian can follow Jesus because His sacrifice made possible our regeneration; His life became ours by the new birth. This gives us the potential of responding to His compelling example as well as to the examples of the prophets.

The suffering and persecution graphically described in Hebrews 11 should encourage us and should save us from morbid introspection or childish self-pity. The prophets' experiences cited there corroborate the Apostle Paul's statement that no testing touches us but that which has afflicted others as well (1 Corinthians 10:13). Hence we can indeed rejoice and be glad when we realize that the saints and the martyrs of the past have been able to *stand*—and we can as well. They suffered, and so shall we; they endured, and so can we. With the apostles we can give thanks that we are counted worthy to suffer shame for Christ's name.

Added to retrospect, prospect completes our perspective. "Great is your reward in heaven." To know about ultimate recompense helps us endure present temptations, testings, and trials. How encouraging to anticipate that the Lord Jesus will someday say to us, "Well done." Our Savior provided a compelling illustration of what our attitude should be in His description of the woman who is about to give birth. She endures the pain of childbirth because of the prospect of bringing a new life into the world.

This truth was brought into sharper focus for me when our oldest child, Carreen, was born. As I observed the pain my wife endured prior to the birth, and then the joy she manifested upon becoming a parent, I was filled with a sense of thanksgiving for my wife and of reverence for the miracle of a new life in our baby girl.

Our Savior thus teaches us that though we encounter difficulty or pain or agony now, afterward comes our great reward in Heaven. So let us rejoice and be glad. Even more, let us make this point of view central to our manner of life. Then we will have a perspective that includes both retrospect and prospect, and we will be able to encourage others, both by exhortation and by exemplification, to share that perspective as well. This demonstration can challenge the believing community to confront tribulation with fortitude and anticipation of blessing and to respond constructively to Biblically informed leadership.

3

Exampling I

*Don't let anyone look down on you because you are
young, but set an example for the believers in speech, in
life, in love, in faith and in purity. Until I come, devote
yourself to the public reading of Scripture, to preaching
and to teaching. Do not neglect your gift, which was given
you through a prophetic message when the body of elders
laid their hands on you. Be diligent in these matters; give
yourself wholly to them, so that everyone may see your
progress. Watch your life and doctrine closely. Persevere in
them, because if you do, you will save both yourself and
your hearers.* (1 Timothy 4:12-16)

Perhaps you can recall playing mimicking games in childhood.
Many people continue this practice as adults, and Christian
leaders sometimes find they are imitated whether for good or
ill. This type of superficial behavior was not what the Apostle Paul
meant when he exhorted his son in the faith to be an example for
believers. Instead, we know from the above verses that Timothy was
called by God to exhibit dynamic spiritual qualities that characterize
the dedicated believer in Christ.

With this in mind, the Christian leader does well to think through the Biblical significance of the term *example*. In the language of the New Testament the word means "type" or "pattern." In those days the word denoted using a sharp instrument to strike the material at hand, perhaps a clay tablet, in order to form a letter or a design. This process eventually resulted in a standard for other items of a similar nature. That is why the Apostle Paul used this word to describe Timothy's being a model to the church. God had molded Timothy into a godly pattern so he could be an example to others.

The Designer in Control

Implicit in the creating of a pattern is the forceful shaping of a substance into a meaningful design. The aggressive efforts of the workman produces this result. First, though, comes the processing.

I am reminded of a young professor living some distance from his family. When his parents queried, "Do you have a good preacher at your church?" the son answered laconically, "Yes." Pressed for a fuller explanation, the young man responded, "Mother and Daddy, we have a very fine preacher. He's gifted, studies hard, is well-versed." Then he paused and said, "But he hasn't suffered enough."

This perceptive young man recognized that although the words were eloquent and the doctrine orthodox, a vital component was missing. To me, the conclusion is inescapable: when you and I are called to be examples, we must expect suffering to be an essential element in our preparation. The divine Designer will strike painful blows as He shapes us into the pattern He has in mind.

From Paul's perspective, Timothy, though comparatively young, showed enough evidence of the shaping process to be an example to other believers. Several observations may be drawn. For instance, the ministry of example does not so much require a chronological component as a developmental one. Leadership is more a matter of quality than of seniority. Thus, those who are younger should not be reluctant to develop characteristics of leadership, recognizing that in the Biblical context the term *youth* need not be synonymous with immaturity. For example, Timothy was not a teenager. One of the church fathers, Irenaeus, indicated that in Timothy's time the term *youth* referred to those up to forty years of age—perhaps because so many leaders at that time were much older. So Timothy may possibly have been at least in his late thirties.

Establishing Creditability

The Christian leader who heeds Paul's instruction to Timothy to be a type or pattern of the believer will establish creditability in our culture at a time when too many seem to be saying, "Do as I say, but don't do as I do." At one time the younger generation would accept such a statement, at least superficially. That day is past. Today's generation needs not only exhortation but also exemplification. Believers observe carefully what a leader does and so determine for themselves his creditability.

Sadly, some graduates of Christian colleges and Bible institutes are not living for God today. Certainly the responsibility for their spiritual drifting lies primarily with them, but some of them became disillusioned with Christianity partly because they saw in the lives of Christian leaders a contradiction between affirmation and action. How important to understand what is involved in being a type or pattern of the believer!

One illustration of belief authenticated by action was that of the Thessalonian Christians. Paul described them as models to all the believers in Macedonia and Achaia (1 Thessalonians 1:7). As Paul continued, he made reference to one of the major ways in which the Thessalonian Christians became an example to believers:

> . . . you turned to God from idols to serve the living and true God, and to wait for his Son from heaven, whom he raised from the dead—Jesus, who rescues us from the coming wrath. (vv. 9, 10)

The True Convert

This succinct statement admirably summarizes what the Bible teaches about conversion. Without question today's Christian leader ought to manifest these characteristics of this transforming experience:

- A past action that was *determinative*: turning to God from idols.
- A present state that should be *normative*: to serve the living and true God.
- A perspective that is *regulative* of our actions and attitudes: to await His Son's return from Heaven.

The past action of turning to God from idols involves repentance toward God as well as faith in our Lord Jesus Christ. One reason we find such a difference between the number of those who make a profession in evangelistic campaigns and the number of those who actually continue on as faithful believers is that some professed conversions do not involve genuine repentance or turning to God from idols. Let me explain.

Too often the gospel presentation leaves out the repudiation of one's own supposed righteousness in favor of God's forgiveness and imputed holiness. For some this results in an endeavor to conclude a bargaining agreement with God akin to that between labor and management. In effect these individuals offer their resources, capabilities, and reputation in return for God's acceptance of them as believers. Others describe salvation as simply an exciting encounter with a dynamic personality. For them the resulting relationship becomes similar to what they have with other human beings, not a unique commitment to Jesus Christ as Lord.

In contrast to this thinking, consider both the preaching of our Lord Jesus Christ and that of His apostles. In Matthew 4:17 we read, "From that time on Jesus began to preach, 'Repent, for the kingdom of heaven is near.'" Immediately after Pentecost Peter preached about the crucifixion and resurrection of Christ and then called on his hearers to repent (Acts 2:38).

This same emphasis may be found in Paul's ministry. To the group gathered to hear him at Mars Hill, he declared that God now "commands all people everywhere to repent" (Acts 17:30). In his valedictory statement to the Ephesian elders Paul testified, "I have declared to both Jews and Greeks that they must turn to God in repentance and have faith in our Lord Jesus" (Acts 20:21).

Clinging to Idols

Some may ask what in particular comprises repentance. I believe the Savior addressed this question in His statement to the crowds traveling with Him as recorded in Luke 14: "If anyone comes to me and does not hate his father and mother, his wife and children, his brothers and sisters—yes, even his own life—he cannot be my disciple" (v. 26). Put another way, He was saying, "You have to turn to Me and must renounce all competing loyalties, whether these be idols of wood or stone, or whether they be parents, wife, or children, or the worship of oneself."

The coldness and barrenness in the lives of professing Christians is sometimes due to a divided allegiance. A superficial "accepting" of Christ permits other commitments to compete for priority. Consequently the individual, as described by the Apostle James, is double-minded and thus unstable in all he does (1:8).

I have talked with people, including long-time believers—some even in Christian work—who have not given up their idols. Too frequently one of these idols is the self-gratification that exacts its tribute in immoral behavior. On the other hand, the more you and I recognize the holiness, righteousness, power, and greatness of God, the more we are moved to repentance. Often through bitter experience we, like the rich young ruler who was reluctant to sell his possessions to follow the Lord (Luke 18:18-23), must learn that God confronts us at precisely the place where we have our idol and demands our renunciation of it as a competing loyalty.

Another key factor in repentance must be the recognition that we have absolutely nothing to contribute to our salvation; we cannot merit or earn it. As the prophet Isaiah so eloquently put it in his prayer: "all our righteous acts are like filthy rags" (Isaiah 64:6). Augustus Toplady has captured this thought in his hymn "Rock of Ages":

> Nothing in my hand I bring,
>   Simply to Thy cross I cling;
> Naked, come to Thee for dress,
>   Helpless, look to Thee for grace;
> Foul, I to the fountain fly,
>   Wash me, Savior, or I die!

A God Who Lives

The second characteristic of conversion, "to serve the living and true God," ought to be the norm for every Christian and should be visible in the life of the Christian leader. This evidence will best be achieved as we understand the significance of the two descriptive words the apostle uses in speaking of God: "living" and "true."

What difference does it make that we are to serve a "living" God? I suggest this makes possible a dynamic relationship, something we could never have with an abstract force or principle. An examination of history provides dramatic instances—some inspiring, some tragic—of incredible devotion and sacrifice for the sake of a dynamic personality. Of infinitely greater significance is our relationship to the living God. At Mars Hill Paul captured the essence of what I have in mind when he said, "'In him we live and move and have our being'" (Acts 17:28), making our relationship to God both ongoing and comprehensive. We are obliged to take this fact into account as we integrate it into our ministry of example.

Again, specific Scriptural teaching helps us understand the significance of serving the living God. From our Lord's teaching in John 14, it is clear that obedience is the key:

"If you love me, you will obey what I command. And I will ask the Father, and he will give you another Counselor to be with you forever—the Spirit of truth. . . . Whoever has my commands and obeys them, he is the one who loves me. He who loves me will be loved by my Father, and I too will love him and show myself to him. . . . If anyone loves me, he will obey my teaching. My Father will love him, and we will come to him and make our home with him." (vv. 15, 16, 17, 21, 23)

In this passage our Lord's words "If you love me, you will obey what I command" are followed immediately by His promise of the abiding presence of the Holy Spirit. Similarly, in verse 21, as we show our love by our obedience, we are blessed by God's love and Christ's disclosure of Himself to us, a spiritual bonding of enormous significance. I can think of no more exalting experience in the Christian life than to mature in love and obedience to the Lord and to be recipients of His blessed presence and love. Like any meaningful intimacy, this disclosure to us is a precious, rather fragile thing that occurs only in the context of abiding love, trust, and obedience.

God's Undisputed Integrity

Having considered the significance of serving the "living" God, what difference does it make that we serve the "true" God? The difference is the integrity of our God. The One we worship is wholly consistent and wholly reliable; His Word is forever settled in Heaven.

The capricious deities of pagan religions, on the other hand, engender anxiety in their worshipers. Such individuals can never be sure they have done all they should have. They fear their gods may change the rules or find some detail their hapless subjects may have overlooked.

Thankfully, our God does not act that way. We may depend upon His integrity as One who always keeps His word. So when we serve the Lord, we do so in the confidence that any intellectual construct about Him can be subjected to the test of truth and never be found wanting.

In this age of relativism and changing standards, therefore, our security rests in the fact that you and I serve the true God. Such was the conviction of the Thessalonian believers. Their conversion experience included a belief in God's revelation to which they could commit themselves unequivocally.

Then in verse 23 of John 14 this teaching culminates in our Savior's promise that in response to our obedience He and the Father will make Their home with us. This remarkable passage teaches us that each of the Persons of the Trinity comes into the life of the trusting and obedient believer. We might say that in such a one the Trinity is increasingly "at home." Yet all of this rests on the fact that we serve a living God.

Thus, in modeling our conversion experience let us ever keep in mind the exquisite parallelism between loving the Lord, keeping His commandments, and enjoying a vital relationship with the Triune God in our lives.

Pausing to Keep Perspective

Finally, conversion means that we "wait for His Son from heaven." Such a perspective lifts us beyond those things that could easily dominate our thinking but shouldn't. Many of us know from experience that the enemy can exploit the increasing acceleration of activity to tempt us to become too preoccupied with the present. Being overly busy can cause us to lose the perspective of waiting for God's Son from Heaven.

In our society, many prefer preoccupation to contemplation. For example, a surprising number of people cannot endure silence and seem afraid to engage in quiet reflection. We commonly see young people walking down the street listening to blaring transistor radios or a cassette plus earphones or driving with the car radio going at full volume. These teenagers seem dependent upon continuous, dominating sound.

Similarly, the first thing some adults do when they enter the house is to turn on the radio or TV so they can have sound or sound plus picture. One wonders whether they too fear silence or contemplative thinking. Apparently they do not want to reflect upon the past or to ponder the future. Even in Christian circles, frantic activism seems a compulsive necessity, justified too often as for "the Lord's sake" when it is really for our own.

A meaningful experience in New England some years ago helped me get this issue in better focus. I was asked to preach at the 200th anniversary of a church in Westminster, Massachusetts. The members of that church did their best to re-create the conditions of the past. They sang using a tuning fork and having each line of a hymn called out before it was sung. People came in the dress of many decades ago. As the preacher, I appeared in a top hat, a cutaway coat, and a shirt with a wing collar.

The congregation had further arranged that I should come into town in a horse and buggy rather than in an automobile. So I went out to the edge of town, climbed into the buggy, and was driven to the church. On the way time seemed to slow. As the horse found his way into town, I was able to observe trees and flowers and to enjoy the countryside. How different from driving a car and having to watch for oncoming traffic and obstacles in the road! In the buggy, without the constraints of automobile driving, I found time for *perspective*.

The Christian needs just such opportunities to contemplate the future, but not in a casual way. The Apostle Paul makes that point clear by using language every parent will understand. He declares we are to wait expectantly for God's Son from Heaven. Parents can remember the evenings when they waited up for the children to come home—and were grateful when they heard them open the door. The Apostle Paul has identified such an expectant attitude as one of the evidences of our conversion. Hence believers who have made a radical break with all other allegiances in favor of a continuing, singular commitment to Jesus Christ wait with eager anticipation for the return of God's Son from Heaven.

Whether we are alive or have died when Christ returns, the perspective remains significant. The Christian leader in particular must have this perspective and will avoid overactivity that precludes thinking about things ultimate as well as things immediate.

There are some practical ways we can achieve this objective. One is to refuse to become overcommitted, to cultivate the ability to say no courteously but firmly. This will require that we conduct an intensive review of what we are doing every week or every month, and then rank these activities in the order of their direct contribution to our major calling in life. We must avoid the delusion that every event to which we are invited requires our attendance. We must exercise discipline regarding the amount of time we spend watching television. We must make a serious, determined effort to schedule events with our spouses and families without failing to leave opportunity to be alone and quiet. This may mean rising before the rest of the family gets up. We must use Scripture and devotional literature to focus our attention on the Lord and His purposes in the world. We must have time for reflective prayer. We must seek to expand our mental and spiritual horizons as we ponder the greatness and goodness of God, both to us personally and to His covenant people. We must resolve that our obedience will be in light of God's present commands and promises and the future triumph of His Kingdom reign.

Such exercises will validate the authenticity of our conversion experience and at the same time make us more perceptive and responsible leaders whose example others can follow.

Back in 1975 the student body president at Wheaton College invited President Ford to visit the campus, and he agreed to come. Other than learning a bit about security on that occasion, I was taught anew about expectation. People stood in lines before daybreak to get into our chapel to see the President. The crowds behind the barriers waited a long time and kept looking down the road. Finally the black limousine pulled up, and President Ford stepped out.

When I recall this incident, I am reminded of the Thessalonian Christians' expectation about the return of Christ. That expectation was rooted in the unchanging precepts of Holy Scripture and was related integrally to their experience with the transforming ministry of the grace of God that enabled them to turn from idols to serve their sovereign Lord. All of this combined to give them a ministry of example.

Let us aspire to this same ministry. Our disillusioned society gropes for authenticity, and even the Christian world longs to see reality corroborate our claims to be truly the Lord's. I submit that genuine repentance, vibrant faith, and earnest expectation will enable us to be leaders who set the example for believers.

4

Exampling II

For your yourselves know how you ought to follow our example. We were not idle when we were with you, nor did we eat anyone's food without paying for it. On the contrary, we worked night and day, laboring and toiling so that we would not be a burden to any of you. We did this, not because we do not have the right to such help, but in order to make ourselves a model for you to follow. For even when we were with you, we gave you this rule: "If a man will not work, he shall not eat." We hear that some among you are idle. They are not busy; they are busybodies. Such people we command and urge in the Lord Jesus Christ, to settle down and earn the bread they eat. And as for you, brothers, never tire of doing what is right.
(2 Thessalonians 3:7-13)

This passage teaches us a significant truth: we leaders are to be examples for believers in the way in which we manage our affairs and assume responsibility for the meeting of our temporal needs, just as Paul did as a leader. Unfortunately, a parasitic attitude sometimes manifests itself in the Christian community. A person with such an attitude expects others to do for him what he should do for himself. This temptation confronts even Christian leaders. As the recipients of the goodness, care, and attention of others—frequently because of eloquence or a dynamic personality—leaders can become lax in meeting their own responsibilities.

Certainly Paul as an apostle could have expected the Thessalonians to take care of him. But he worked to meet his needs in order to give the Thessalonians an example of godly self-reliance and consistency. Thus they saw him as a model—a person who worked to support himself just as they were expected to do.

The question naturally arises whether or not we should accept favors or commendation from others. Because of their personality or temperament, some find it difficult to do this. When they are commended for doing a good job, they respond by depreciating their performance. After a while it sounds as though they are encouraging others to make an even stronger case in their favor until finally they have ample justification in agreeing. Others may find it difficult to receive a gift without doing something for their benefactor in return. Ideally we should cultivate a proper balance that accepts deserved praise gracefully but does not presume upon the kindness and consideration of others. This means that obedient Christians will be scrupulous in the way they take care of their personal affairs and will provide an example of self-reliance and dependability while at the same time graciously accepting legitimate tokens of respect and affection.

No Special Favors Warranted

While serving a church in Brockton, Massachusetts, I opened an account at a men's clothing store. The salesman told me the firm would give me the usual clergy discount, but then remarked that some of the local ministers, when called to another parish, had left without paying their bills even though they had been given special consideration. Thus while the store was willing to open an account for a clergyman, they understandably were not enthusiastic about doing so.

I received a somewhat similar reaction from a Christian businessman in the Chicago area. He said that whenever he did business with a man who carried a New Testament in his vest pocket he had to be particularly careful in assessing the transaction. A series of disillusioning experiences had regrettably driven him to the conclusion that a symbolic allegiance to the Bible did not necessarily guarantee business integrity.

Unfortunately, unfavorable reports about some ministers and some Christians in business can be documented. Apparently these individuals presume that our culture expects individuals to try to get something for nothing or to negotiate a questionable transaction or to leave unpaid bills since others can afford to make up the loss. Let me say as forcefully as possible that such practices have no Biblical justification whatsoever. On the contrary, the Apostle Paul's exhortation to work and to eat our own bread applies to paying our accounts in full and seeing to it that our business dealings are scrupulously honest.

Exemplary behavior in business matters will convey both to our fellow Christians and to non-Christians what it means to be a believer. It will also help to offset the attitude of some non-Christians who say they do not want to become Christians because they cannot trust believers as much as they can trust some of their non-Christian friends. Sadly, there is enough truth in this statement to warrant corrective action, particularly if the problem occurs in the life of a Christian leader.

I remember being asked by a prominent Christian to give an address. I drove quite a distance to speak to the group. When I left, the leader shook my hand and said, "You'll be hearing from me." To this day I have heard nothing from him, not even a word of explanation that funds were unavailable for travel expenses or for an honorarium.

Christian leaders ought to recognize that others notice such behavior and are disillusioned by it. On the other hand, when we remember our commitments and honor our obligations, our example confirms our message.

The Godhead Exemplifies Work

Some Christians would agree with all of this and yet conclude that work itself is the result of the Fall and is thus associated with the curse of sin. What they overlook is that God Himself set a pattern of creative work followed by rest (Genesis 1:1—2:3). Further, even before the Fall man was assigned work. Genesis 2:15 says, "The Lord God took the man and put him in the Garden of Eden to work it and take care of it." Thus, while man's survival in a fallen world involves demanding and time-consuming effort, this does not justify the conclusion that all work is the product of the Fall. Nor is it correct to assume that the rest promised us in Hebrews 4 invalidates the legitimacy of work as a fulfillment of our calling as God's servants (cf. 1 Corinthians 15:58). Indeed, the example set for us by the persons of the Godhead corroborates the apostle's teaching about work. Scripture frequently documents the conclusion that God has not ceased His meaningful and purposeful activity in the world.

An example of this teaching may be found in John 5. When the Jews persecuted Jesus for healing on the Sabbath, He responded, "My Father is always at his work to this very day, and I, too, am working" (v. 17). One illustration of the Father's work is mentioned in verse 21, where Jesus declares that the Father raises the dead and gives them life. Then in verse 22 Jesus states that the Father has entrusted the work of judgment to the Son. Similarly, in John 16 the work of the Holy Spirit is described (guiding the disciples into all truth and convicting the world of guilt in regard to sin, righteousness, and judgment).

One of the remarkable aspects of the Holy Spirit's work of convicting the world involves us, as seen in the text of verses 7 and 8, something brought to my attention by a gifted minister some years ago. Our Savior said that the Holy Spirit would be sent to His disciples and would then convict the world; obviously those possessing the Spirit are the ones God uses to participate in His work of conviction. What a challenging thought! I believe that our part involves not only the proclamation of God's truth but also its exemplification. These together comprise a powerful statement to this age. Surely this is a vital part of the ministry of example. Moreover, it is a legitimate aspect of our calling, one which deserves our thoughtful consideration.

Our Calling/Vocation

Divine calling is one of the major themes of the Bible. Probably the best-known aspect of this teaching relates to our salvation. Not as well known but nevertheless very significant is the fact that God also calls us to special service or ministry for Him. Most Christians would agree that such a calling applies to those summoned by God to be ministers or missionaries, but the Biblical teaching is more comprehensive. As we shall see, God calls His people to a variety of functions both in the church and in society. *Both*

One of the earliest indications of our vocation is in what is generally known as the "creation mandate." In Genesis 1:28 God blessed the newly created human beings and then instructed them to subdue the earth and rule over the creatures He had made. In Genesis 2:15 this was applied particularly to the Garden—man's first home:

> The Lord God took the man and put him in the Garden of Eden to work it and take care of it.

Remember that sin had not yet entered the creation; yet the cultivation and keeping of it was mandated by God. Therefore, the general principle of divine calling to meaningful work is not an outcome of the Fall but is rather an application of the "creation mandate" *before* the Fall. Whatever particularization we have of that mandate in our complex and diverse society today, we can go back to this generalization found at the beginning of human history.

Becoming Aware of Gifts

Another basic principle that undergirds our calling to vocation is found in the Great Commission. In Matthew 28:18-20 we are instructed not only to proclaim the gospel, but also to teach disciples to obey everything Christ has commanded. Properly understood, this includes obeying specific moral and ethical imperatives and also responsible stewardship of the gifts God has given to us to use for His glory.

Such stewardship is two-dimensional. From 1 Corinthians 12 and Romans 12 we learn that God the Holy Spirit assigns and equips us for our function as members of the Body of Christ. These passages make clear that the ministry of every believer is vital to the effective functioning of the group as a whole. And 1 Corinthians 7:17-24 instructs us about the place in life the Lord assigns to us and our responsibility to keep God's commands in that situation, whatever our social or economic position, as mandated by our sovereign God.

The immediate question posed by those who accept these truths, however, is how to ascertain God's calling for us in the church and in society. One criterion might be our natural gifts and capabilities. Yet there are instances in which Scripture suggests that God's calling may include His giving us special gifts. Recall that Moses was called of God to lead His people out of Egypt, but protested that he lacked the necessary ability for the task (Exodus 4:10-13). Yet the record of the encounters Moses and Aaron had later with Pharaoh shows that God provided the capabilities commensurate with the calling. Another illustration may be found in Exodus 31, where we read that Bezalel and Oholiab and the other craftsmen were filled "with the Spirit of God, with skill, ability and knowledge in all kinds of crafts" (see vv. 3 and 6). In still other instances, such as in the lives of Paul and

Apollos, scholarship and eloquence were natural gifts God transformed after calling His servants into ministry.

Furthermore, there are factors other than natural gifts to be taken into account in ascertaining the calling of God. From the Biblical illustrations of Abraham and Moses and others we know that one key element can be direct revelation from God. This may come to the individual or to a group regarding one of their associates. In the Old Testament, for example, Samuel received a revelation from God concerning David's kingship (1 Samuel 16:1-13). And in the New Testament a group of prophets and teachers perceived the Holy Spirit's guidance regarding the ministry of two of their members, Barnabas and Saul (Acts 13:1, 2).

An important factor, therefore, is the perspective of a trusted fellow believer or of a fellowship with which an individual may be associated. Such an insight may either affirm or restrain a proposed action and thus provide a balance to what on occasion can be inordinate subjectivism.

In my experience another major means God has used has been circumstances. Incidents ranging from the Communist takeover of China (which prevented my wife and me from going there as missionaries) to unsolicited opportunities for ministry have helped me see the sovereign hand of God controlling and guiding in my vocational assignments.

As a general rule we should walk through open doors that are not such because of manipulation or the invoking of special privilege but because God has so ordered it.

Also important in an assessment of our calling is the recognition that we may have several responsibilities at one time. In my case, I was called of God to be a husband and father as well as a church member and an educator. One of the most difficult tasks a Christian leader faces is the achievement of a proper balance. Far too frequently sufficient time and energy are not reserved for spouse and family, with the result that success in the most visible calling is sadly offset by tragic failure in this other very important responsibility.

I recommend a rigorous appraisal of the total schedule so that, as I told my successor at Wheaton College, our families will not be left with only the tattered fragments of our emotional and spiritual resources. Just as God evaluates our stewardship of time and opportunities, He will assess this aspect of our lives as well.

Obeying God's Commandments

Such assessment should be viewed in the larger context of God's judgment of His people. Taking this prospect into account seems absent from the thinking of many believers who assume that forgiveness and restoration after failure or deliberate wrongdoing ends the matter. To be sure, the Lord promises that His people's sins and iniquities will be remembered no more. But I believe this refers to our acceptance in God's sight and must be viewed alongside other Scriptures that address not our eternal status as children of God but our stewardship as servants of God. Our accountability in this latter category has both immediate and ultimate consequences depending upon whether we have obeyed or ignored God's commandments.

Along these lines the usual understanding of the Third Commandment of the Decalogue is that we should avoid swearing because this takes the Lord's name in vain. That is true, but taking the Lord's name in vain also occurs when we publicly confess we are His and yet act in a careless, slipshod, or dishonest way so as to discredit His name. Scripture records a number of instances when God judged servants who failed to glorify Him. The incident of Moses' disobedience in Numbers 20:1-12 is an example. You will recall that God told him to speak to the rock to bring water for the people. Instead, in frustration and anger he struck the rock with his staff and was held accountable by God for his disobedience. This failure brought drastic consequences.

Long-term Accountability

Consider also the principle set forth in Galatians 6:7, 8—we shall surely reap what we sow. Again we must differentiate between forgiveness and consequences. In Numbers 14 God forgave Israel so that they were not totally destroyed, but they had to wander for forty years in the desert as a consequence of their rebellion. Simple logic tells us that a person coming to Christ at age seventy will not be given a new start at age twenty, but will live with the consequences of the wasted years. Those forgiven for immoral behavior sadly are never again virginal. The fallen Christian leaders of our day, thank God, may be forgiven, but the mental and emotional scars their families and associates have endured will never be fully eradicated in this life.

Let us also remember that accountability continues into eternity. For one of the most graphic descriptions of this teaching see 1 Corinthians 3:11-15, where the Apostle Paul characterizes our works as gold, silver, and costly stones, or as wood, hay, or straw, with all to be tested by fire. The passage makes clear, as in Galatians 6, that we have a choice. In this case we select the materials with which to build upon the foundation. Probably for most of us there will be a mixture of that which will endure the test by fire and that which will not. Calling on God for His help, we should ensure that we build as much as possible with "gold, silver [and] costly stones."

I imagine that the day of ultimate accountability will be one of high drama. For some it will be a final vindication of faithful service, though they may have had no formal recognition during their lifetimes. For others it will be a shattering surprise to see a carefully crafted but self-serving edifice reduced to ashes.

To the degree to which you and I may have the experience of seeing some of our earthly activities accounted as worthless in God's sight, our reaction could well be grief and remorse. I suggest that this may be why reference is made to tears in Heaven (see Isaiah 25:8 and Revelation 21:4). If my inference is correct, we will at last see our lives from God's perspective and will realize how much more sowing to the

Spirit we could have done and how much more building with enduring materials we could have done as well. Our loving Heavenly
Father, in one of the most touching scenes in the Bible, will then wipe
away our tears (see the above references). The assessment has been
completed, and yet we are accepted in the Beloved.

And What of Others?

For me, the prospect of divine assessment is a stimulus to excellence
and an antidote for indolence. In addition, our experience of God's
love powerfully motivates us to "climb the steep ascent of Heaven
through peril, toil and pain." The challenge to the Christian leader
from the Reginald Heber hymn from which I just quoted is this:
"Who follows in our train?"

I believe our example of accountability can summon others to this
kind of life. They will need to see specific, tangible instances, however, to assure them that what we propose is practicable.

Take the matter of financial support for the Christian leader.
Scripture teaches that the laborer is worthy of his hire and that provision should be made for those who minister (1 Timothy 5:17, 18).
Yet the situation in New Testament times called for voluntary
restraint on the Apostle Paul's part. Perhaps this was due to abuses
of the practice of sharing reported in Acts 4:32-35. Possibly this not
only reduced the Jerusalem church to poverty, but also may have
caused the Thessalonian church to have a problem with some who
wanted sustenance but refused to work for it (see 2 Thessalonians
3:10-15). Writing to this church, Paul explained why he refused support that legitimately was his in order to be an example of voluntary
discipline in working to sustain himself. How refreshing! Rather than
becoming an excuse for some to develop an unjustified dependency
on other believers, he wanted those able to do so to work in a disciplined manner. He addressed his rebuke not to those who for one reason or another *could* not work but to those who found work
distasteful.

Accountability also includes changing our practice in order to avoid helping others justify their harmful excesses. My German grandfather was one who willingly gave up what he considered a right for this reason. He believed beverage alcohol was one of God's good gifts if used in moderation. However, when he joined his daughter in Winslow, Arizona, he learned that among the Indians of that area alcohol abuse was widespread, causing all kinds of personal and family problems. In light of this, my grandfather never touched another drop of beverage alcohol.

Every decision of any consequence that a believer makes, therefore, ought to be an examined decision. On occasion we will voluntarily give up a right to a practice that under other circumstances we would consider acceptable. Similarly, as leaders you and I must not take advantage of others for our sustenance, but should work to make provision for ourselves rather than succumb to indolence.

A resource God has ordained to help ensure accountability—namely, church discipline—is sometimes not utilized. Such discipline should be exercised in cases involving moral lapses, but a church that has a clear understanding of Biblical doctrine must also discipline those who are dilatory in making provisions for themselves and their families. This important task must not be shirked. The non-Christian world may not see us in our Christian worship, but cannot fail to notice our behavior where work is performed.

I learned early aboard ship that my fellow officers cared little about my rhetoric concerning my beliefs or my love for Christ or the Bible on my desk. What got their attention and respect was my professional competency. They wanted to be assured that my men were ready for action. When I had responsibility on the bridge as Officer of the Deck, could I keep the ship where it was supposed to be? Only then were my associates ready to listen to my testimony.

As we respond to and live out the divine calling to our work may we magnify and glorify the name of our Lord, not just by the phrases we utter—as important as they are—but by the quality and integrity of the work we perform.

Our Work Goes On

Finally, we will have work to do in eternity, and this will be commensurate, I believe, with the level of our spiritual competency in this life. We see in 2 Timothy 2:10-12 that the quality of our commitment now has a bearing upon the assignment we will receive as we reign with Christ in our glorified state. And the song of the celestial beings in Revelation 5:9, 10 includes the declaration that Christ has made the redeemed "to be a kingdom and priests to serve our God, and they will reign on the earth." In Revelation 2:26, 27 it seems clear that this responsibility is linked to the degree to which individuals have overcome and have done the Savior's will to the end. A similar thought is expressed in Revelation 20:4, 6 and 22:5.

It is challenging to recognize that God calls us to glorify Him, to edify our fellow believers, to be a witness in the world, and to prepare for the continuing responsibilities that will be ours in His eternal Kingdom. In a remarkable way the tranquillity and order of the creation before the Fall will be restored through Christ's redemptive work, and we will participate meaningfully in His triumph over the whole creation. Surely we have no more compelling apologetic for work and for accountability than this.

$\overline{5}$

Exampling III

A s Christian leaders we have been called to the ministry of exampling. What kind of a life are we to live as we fulfill that calling?

The Call to Purity and Integrity

Inextricably intertwined with the creditability of our conversion experience and our calling (vocation) is the quality of our manner of life and our purity and integrity in personal practice. The Apostle Paul's challenge to Timothy to "set an example for the believers . . . in life . . . in purity" (1 Timothy 4:12) stands in vivid contrast to his eloquent characterization of those who live as enemies of the cross of Christ:

> For, as I have often told you before and now say again even with tears, many live as enemies of the cross of Christ. Their destiny is destruction, their god is their stomach, and their glory is in their shame. Their mind is on earthly things. (Philippians 3:18, 19)

Paul's assessment was the natural outgrowth of his convictions regarding the position of the redeemed in Christ ("our citizenship is in heaven," v. 20a). This perspective enabled him to be realistic about others following the pattern they observed in him and in his associates (v. 17). Paul said he put no confidence in the flesh, then contrasted this walk of consecration with that which is generally descriptive of the day in which you and I live and which was true also of the age of the Apostle Paul.

Paul's teaching was not about the pagan world but rather about those who in a formal, confessional sense wanted to number themselves with the believing community. They decided to bear the name of Christ—but only in a selective way. They sought to extract from their identification with His name those things appropriate to their own lifestyle and their own needs. Deeply burdened, Paul wept as he called such persons "enemies of the cross of Christ." Apparently they wanted to identify with Christ but not with His cross. We must recognize that in any discussion of consecration or dedication as part of the ministry of example, we are dealing with a distinction even within the believing community at large—some follow Christ in truth, some on their own terms.

In Paul's calling certain believers "enemies of the cross of Christ," the choice of words is crucial. We hear, for example, of persons who regard their Christian experience as not dependent upon Jesus' death on the cross but based solely on their having had a dynamic, meaningful encounter with Him as a great personality. Such a superficial outlook is temporary and provisional and can always be superseded by another, more dynamic meaningful encounter.

Genuine consecration is not rooted simply in the personal attractiveness of Jesus, but is an important outcome of His saving work on the cross. Not only is the believer brought out of darkness into light, but the cross becomes a working principle that informs the entire life of the redeemed person.

Keeping the Cross Paramount

The future is bleak indeed for those who do not recognize the cross of Christ as paramount in their lives. "Their destiny is destruction, their god is their stomach, and their glory is in their shame." Such results inexorably follow a capitulation to profligacy; unbridled experience becomes the primary criterion and dominant force. This is the thrust of the apostle's statement. He portrays a physiological inversion of the human being. Think about it. The visceral and, sadly, the genital take precedence over the cerebral and spiritual because the human being is dominated by urges, passions, and drives. All of these are God-given and legitimate, but only when they are controlled within Biblically defined moral guidelines.

Live Life Through Script

The microphone and the lights in a conference area are available to the participants because of the controlled use of electricity. But if a thunderstorm occurs while a person is out walking in the forest under the trees, he may suffer a fatal accident. Why? That same electricity unharnessed can have wildly destructive influence. So it is with human beings.

For example, some wrongly insist they are part of the believing community, but seek to justify sexual practices forbidden by the Scriptures. This rationalization seems to be based upon two assumptions: first, that God made some human beings with different sexual desires and will not condemn them for seeking the satisfaction of those desires; and second, that the Bible condemns only promiscuous or exploitative sexual relationships but not long-term, responsible ones, even if they are homosexual.

Such an approach to Scripture is based on an incomplete view of all that the Bible teaches on the subject and on an assumption about human nature which fails to recognize the effects of sin upon it. Thus this view seriously falls short of the truth.

Evil Thoughts, Evil Actions

The undisciplined leader fails in the ministry of example not only by convoluted thinking that results in distortions of Biblical principles, but also by evil thoughts that culminate in evil actions. In the Sermon on the Mount the Lord Jesus spoke about purity of thought, saying, "You have heard that it was said, 'Do not commit adultery.' But I tell you that anyone who looks at a woman lustfully has already committed adultery with her in his heart" (Matthew 5:27, 28). Further, Matthew 15:19 declares that evil thoughts lead to adulterous deeds. As surely as night follows day, evil thoughts will result in evil actions.

Even within the Christian community people fail to realize that what they think, hear, see, and read can seriously compromise their example. I once knew some Christians who went to Chicago to see an X-rated movie. They said they needed to be aware of what such movies portrayed. Perhaps they returned unaffected by that experience, but I doubt it. Such experiences are not necessary in order for us to be well-informed, particularly at the expense of a sullied mind.

I remember visiting an officer aboard another ship while I was overseas during World War II. The first time I came to see him he was expecting me. The next week I came back unexpectedly and found he had put back on the bulkheads the pictures he had taken down before my first visit. The pictures were calculated to incite lust. I could not help wondering what effect these pictures were having upon him or upon his shipmates who came to his stateroom.

Is it possible for a Christian to have a manner of life antithetical to what a believer's manner of life should be like? Regrettably it is indeed possible. When the Apostle Paul enumerates the works of the flesh in Galatians 5:19-21, it seems evident he is indicating the possibility that Christians can do such things. Otherwise, there would have been no point in his saying, "Live by the Spirit, and you will not gratify the desires of the sinful nature" (v. 16).

Paul emphasizes that the Spirit and the sinful nature (the flesh) are in conflict with each other so that we do not do what we want to do (see also Romans 7:14-23). One interpretation of this passage in Galatians is that we cannot do the good things we want to do because of the opposition of our flesh. The other view, which I prefer, is that as we yield to the enabling presence of the Holy Spirit, we do not do the things we might naturally want to do because He is there to restrain and control.

A reading of 1 and 2 Corinthians reveals that the man discussed in 1 Corinthians 5 had confessed Jesus Christ as Savior and had been admitted to the fellowship of the church (see v. 2). Yet he had engaged in a sexual sin that the apostle said was not practiced even among the pagans!

In response to Paul's rebuke, the Corinthian church disciplined that member. Second Corinthians 2:3-11 mentions a believer who repented and was restored. I believe the individual to whom the Apostle Paul referred was the same man mentioned in 1 Corinthians 5. If so, this account confirms the view that the Christian may choose to go the way of the flesh. The wonderful thing is that he does not *need* to adopt such a manner of life because he can choose to live under the power and guidance of the Holy Spirit and thus be controlled by the Spirit rather than by the flesh.

Self-gratification Not Limited to Sex

Christian leaders face incredible assaults from temptations that are not only sexual but span the whole range of self-indulgence. When Scripture speaks of certain believers' god being their appetite (Philippians 3:19), it is saying that whether the preoccupation is with material things or creature comforts or sex or fame or power, there is a capitulation to the insatiable appetite for self-gratification.

Some time ago a gifted preacher came to visit us, and we went out with mutual friends for a meal. Throughout the evening this man dominated the conversation, orienting it again and again toward himself. His preoccupation with his own interests became painfully obvious. Not too many months later he left the ministry because in his desire for self-gratification he had engaged in immorality.

This misguided brother had permitted his appetites to become his god. They dominated him. He had allowed himself to be turned upside-down morally; the spiritual was subordinated to the physical and emotional. Sadly, his case is not unique. Christian leaders are subject to this kind of temptation to an exceptional degree because some people are always prepared to indulge the leader in one way or another if he will allow it.

The well-publicized failure of leaders in student work and in tel-evangelism underscores our need to be alert to danger signals in our lives. Frequently the leader who becomes overcommitted and emotionally spent is unusually vulnerable to temptation. Weariness weakens our defenses.

Another process that can lead to disaster is to become overly dependent upon affirmation and praise. Then when a colleague or a spouse is more realistic and calls our attention to a fault in us, perhaps thoughtlessness or neglect, we are tempted to reject this, preferring the fantasy some admirers are quite prepared to nurture. Such a self-deceived leader is likely to fall into the trap of believing that the admirer is the only one who really understands and truly appreciates the leader's qualities. Like Narcissus, he is headed for disaster.

Tragically a leader's failure inevitably affects not only himself but his ministry and his family. While we thank God for forgiveness and restoration, we often overlook the fact that the hurt and disillusionment in other lives is remarkably persistent and damaging.

Yielding to temptation in these ways offends God and damages His witness in the world and negatively impacts others. That is why the Scriptures sternly warn against giving in to temptation:

> Do not be deceived: God cannot be mocked. A man reaps what he sows. The one who sows to please his sinful nature, from that nature will reap destruction; the one who sows to please the Spirit, from the Spirit will reap eternal life. (Galatians 6:7, 8)

The Necessity of Self-Discipline

To control self-gratification, the Christian leader must learn to practice self-discipline. He can start simply. A certain man determined to eat only potatoes for thirty days. Another man, learning of this exercise, decided he would do the same with peanut butter and buttermilk for the same period of time. Though tests of this kind can be legalistic and self-serving, I know from personal experience that they can also help develop self-control.

After graduating from Wheaton College, I went to Clark University in Massachusetts for graduate study. I had been awarded a scholarship with a stipend that allowed for lunch and dinner six days a week. Because I felt the need for a daily breakfast as well, I used the small amount of money I had to buy each week a box of shredded wheat, a can of condensed milk, and a pound of brown sugar. For two semesters I had the same breakfast each morning: shredded wheat, brown sugar, condensed milk.

I confess it was some years before I could enjoy shredded wheat again, but the discipline dictated by my lack of funds was good for me. I believe I appreciated my education more. And later I certainly valued the more varied breakfasts I was able to afford.

Yet this example raises an issue of self-indulgence. If we can afford to eat large quantities of rich foods, should we do so? Long before the medical profession urged moderation and balance in our diets, the Bible condemned gluttony (see Proverbs 23:19-21). Slowly we are learning that a proper diet contributes to our well-being, but overindulgence can give us serious health problems.

Moreover, we need to recognize the spiritual benefits of what at first seems to have no bearing on our ongoing relationship with God. Consider, for example, a regular program of moderate exercise. Such a routine requires discipline, but it is also simply good stewardship of the temple of the Holy Spirit—our body. More and more, modern medicine is speaking about the interrelationship of body, mind, and spirit. Let us develop discipline in diet and exercise before such a regimen is forced upon us by a heart attack—if we survive. It has been my experience that such discipline permits us to function far more effectively spiritually as well as physically and mentally.

Admittedly the discipline just considered involves primarily the physical. More critical is the self-discipline of the mind, which is where the initial struggle takes place. Our football coach at Wheaton College used to tell his players, "You give up first in your mind; then your body quits." Similarly we give up first in our minds, and then we actually engage in self-indulgence, whether for material possessions or fame or gluttony or sex or whatever we think we must have. Discipline of the mind produces disciplined behavior. The Christian leader who has integrity controls his mind so he is not overcome by temptation or is adversely affected by externals.

Those who endeavor to be examples for believers in manner of life will not be like a man I recall who was a fellow attendee at a White House conference for Christian leaders. I saw an expensive limousine parked in front of the White House and assumed it was for the use of a government official or even the President. It was not. This private vehicle, complete with chauffeur, was for the man I mentioned, who forcefully and repeatedly pled for funds to support his ministry.

I struggled with that. I knew of persons who helped to provide that leader's support out of their modest retirement income. If you and I, for ego status and reinforcement, need the kind of accoutrements that are extravagant and have no justification other than our own personal gratification, we too have made a god of our selfish desires and appetites (Philippians 3:19).

The "gospel of success" so popular today says that if you are an obedient believer you will not only be healthy but also wealthy and powerful. Such a so-called gospel overlooks many explicit statements of the Holy Scriptures. True, some believers have succeeded or enjoyed monetary riches, but others have not. Can you imagine telling John the Baptist and the scores of saints listed in Hebrews 11, "Well, if you had had more faith or if you had been more dedicated, you would have had more blessings and less suffering"? Nonsense.

At the same time, we need to be careful to avoid the erroneous belief that there is something inherently evil about having possessions and enjoying them. Abraham was both rich and pleasing to God. But I believe God challenges us, as leaders who are also disciples, to model the kind of lifestyle mentioned by the Apostle Paul in 1 Timothy 6:6-10. What will be sufficient to enable us to be content? Clearly the love of money will *not* bring about this result. Yet our culture uses every device possible to induce us to contradict a spiritual manner of life by indulging in materialistic excess. As believers and as Christian leaders we should manifest a way of life free from the tyranny of credit cards, crushing debt, and inordinate worry over material possessions.

Further, the practice of questioning our expenditures or the way in which we use our time will in reality liberate us to focus on ministry that is oriented outward rather than constantly inward. A good question to ask is, what long-term consequences will result from our behavior pattern, both as far as we personally are concerned and as far as those who follow us are concerned?

I continue to appreciate the needful bit of homely wisdom I received from a man who for some years was chairman of the board of Gordon College—wisdom about not putting my confidence in the praise of others. When I was leaving Gordon to go to Wheaton College, the president asked me to preach the baccalaureate sermon, something that he usually did himself. I considered it a great honor, and I prepared diligently for the occasion. After the service people came to me to offer their congratulations. Then this gentlemen commented, "Thank you for a good message. Now let me share something with you. Don't forget that praise is like horse liniment." I did not understand what he meant, so I asked him to explain. With a twinkle in his eye he answered, "Praise may be useful as long as it isn't taken internally!" Pride is a danger for all of us.

The Difference Between Position and Practice

The Christian leader who would exemplify a pure, disciplined manner of life must each day make the choice to walk in the Spirit and not in the flesh, and this is possible only because in Christ he has been redeemed. The words that Scripture uses for *redemption* also referred in that day to purchasing slaves out of the slave market and setting them free. Scripture repeatedly makes the point that once this happens, the Christian increasingly should make true in experience what is true positionally:

> You were taught, with regard to your former way of life, to put off your old self, which is being corrupted by its deceitful desires; to be made new in the attitude of your minds; and to put on the new self, created to be like God in true righteousness and holiness. (Ephesians 4:22-24)

I learned the difference between position and practice when I entered the Navy during World War II. I was what was called in those days a "ninety-day wonder." Four years of college and ninety days of naval training made us naval officers positionally. But unfortunately a one-day cruise down the Hudson River on a patrol craft was all the sea duty we had experienced.

After commissioning, I was to report to the *USS Wichita* on December 3, 1942. On the train from New York to Norfolk, a sailor who had frequented the bar on the train saluted me and asked my judgment on a matter. I was impressed by how much that single gold stripe meant. But once aboard ship it was an entirely different situation. Then the theory had to be put into practice. My division officer and his men looked condescendingly at me while I tried to remember what I had read about the main features of a combatant ship. I was really struggling, and they all knew it.

The next three months were extraordinarily painful for me because I was seasick and homesick. But I had to make good in practice what I was in position. After all, I was a commissioned officer in the Unites States Navy!

A Neutral Position Untenable

Part of what is involved in making our position good in practice involves not yielding our capabilities unto sin. Instead, we must take positive action and not try to stay in a position of neutrality, which is impossible. In taking this step, the believer would do well to consider carefully a very interesting and significant statement we may tend to miss:

> . . . offer yourselves to God, as those who have been brought from death to life; and offer the parts of your body to him as instruments of righteousness. (Romans 6:13)

Do you know what sometimes happens when we attempt to establish a manner of life pleasing to God? We reverse the sequence of Scripture and yield our *capabilities* to God before we submit *ourselves* to Him. The results are predictable. Because we have not yielded ourselves to God, we find the yielding of our capabilities to be spasmodic or incomplete. Since our basic commitment is tentative or absent, the willingness to place our capabilities unreservedly at the disposal of the Lord is subject to the whims of the moment.

Let it be recognized, then, that to be an example in our manner of life demands the decisive subordination of ourselves to Christ. We will then offer our specific gifts to the Lord as a logical product of our commitment. The Christian leader should refuse to limit his consecration to the yielding of his *abilities* as instruments of righteousness. Instead, as he yields *himself* to God and then places his abilities at God's disposal, he is ready to be used constructively in the fellowship of God's people.

Results Not Necessarily Quantitative

As we dedicate both ourselves and our capabilities to the Savior, we must exercise caution in our attempts to evaluate our ministry. The tendency to use only a quantitative measurement leads to errors in judgment. God's criterion is *quality*. As we have discussed earlier, the testing agent is the fire of God's judgment (1 Corinthians 3:10-15). Wide-ranging achievements mean nothing without quality results.

Having resolved to glorify God in his body, soul, and spirit because by redemption these are God's, the leader is then liberated to serve God's people wherever he is sent, without regard for status or personal reward.

I once knew of a young man who had completed his high school education more by his personality and his athletic prowess than by his academic achievements. But the system that had worked so successfully for him in high school failed in college, and low grades forced his withdrawal. But the shock of his experience brought him to his senses; he eventually finished both college and seminary and entered the ministry. In time he became pastor of a thriving church that under his leadership grew in numbers and resources. Then one day he announced his resignation. The people of the church were bewildered and wondered if he was not being paid enough or if he needed more privileges and benefits. On the contrary, they found he had accepted a call to a much smaller church in a far more obscure location and at a lower salary. His explanation was simple: God had called him, and he was obeying that call.

This wise young pastor had determined that he would do the will of God without regard to perquisites or prominence. As I heard this, I was both refreshed and challenged. Here is an illustration of a believer who yielded himself to the Lord and put his abilities at God's disposal, leaving it up to his Heavenly Father to judge the quality of his efforts.

A Singular Loyalty

Continuing to make good in practice what we are in position involves a constant attention to purity. This freedom from defilement encompasses more than avoiding evil thoughts (which do inevitably lead to evil actions). Purity also conveys the idea of that which is unadulterated, such as a singular loyalty that allows no other commitment. Our commitment is first of all to the Lord rather than to our career or our own well-being or any other cause.

One way to discover whether such commitment is present in a given individual is to observe his work habits between the time he submits his resignation from an organization and the time he actually leaves it. Those with a purity of commitment will give full measure until the last day; others will not. Or consider those who claim to be called to a work, but then leave at the first sign of difficulty or when offered a higher salary elsewhere. Clearly the commitment was in fact tentative or provisional and was based on dollars or ease rather than dedication.

Purity Extends to Groups

The example of purity that we set as individuals should be true also of the groups or organizations or churches of which we are a part. This expectation is vividly portrayed in Scripture.

Consider, for example, the message Isaiah the prophet brought to Israel from their sovereign God. Throughout the first chapter of his prophecy Isaiah eloquently conveyed the Lord's indictment and emphasized the concepts of purity we have already considered. In verses 2-4 commitment is lacking in God's people as a group. They continued to observe the forms of worship (vv. 11-15), but God knew they were insincere and thus rejected their overtures. Further, this compromise of their commitment produced unclean behavior (vv. 16, 21-23). God's people were supposed to be examples to the nations around them, an expectation pictured in 2:2-5. This appeal to Israel and Judah affirmed the principle that singularity of commitment would prevent the sullying of practices.

We see the same emphasis with respect to the New Testament church. Paul explains that the manifold wisdom of God is to be made known to the rulers and authorities in the heavenly realms through the church (Ephesians 3:10, 11) and through the witness of God's servants to all people everywhere (vv. 8, 9).

A careful reading of the New Testament epistles will show that the same emphases urged upon Israel and Judah have been directed to the redeemed community bearing the name of Christ. And throughout the centuries of church history the issue of purity persists, with revival/renewal restoring the church to its ministry of example, which rests upon individual loyalty to Christ and uncompromising obedience to His Word. Hence we have a dual responsibility to personal and corporate purity in order to fulfill our calling.

The yielding of the self to Christ, making death with Him the working principle that informs the whole life of the redeemed individual, was Paul's desire when he said, "For to me, to live is Christ . . ." (Philippians 1:21). Such a life effectively and succinctly answers those who ask, "Why didn't God call more brilliant and powerful people?" Simply put, He desires followers fully committed to Him. Part of the impact of our example, shown by the level of our consecration, will be manifested in such commitment. Then those who follow us will not place their trust in our brilliance or eloquence but rather in Christ and His cross and in the sovereign power of our Almighty God.

6

Love

When the characteristics of leaders are enumerated, love is not usually included. Yet this quality is central to the Christian life and to the Christian leader. The following Scriptures make the point:

> One of them, an expert in the law, tested him [Jesus] with this question: "Teacher, which is the greatest commandment in the Law?" Jesus replied: "'Love the Lord your God with all your heart and with all your soul and with all your mind.' This is the first and greatest commandment. And the second is like it: 'Love your neighbor as yourself.'" (Matthew 22:35-39)

[handwritten: Key]

[handwritten: On These Two]

> Dear friends, let us love one another, for love comes from God. Everyone who loves has been born of God and knows God. Whoever does not love does not know God, because God is love. This is how God showed his love among us: He sent his one and only Son into the world that we might live through him. This is love: not that we loved God, but that he loved us and sent his Son as an atoning sacrifice for our sins. Dear friends, since God so loved us, we also ought to love one another. (1 John 4:7-11)

"I just *love* ice cream!" someone might exclaim. This is warm affection, but it is not love. Nor is love a benign glow radiating to all mankind. The word *love* has been so bandied about, misconstrued, and trivialized that attempting to understand the cultural definition of the term, let alone the Biblical one, is difficult.

In previous eras of the church's history, various aspects of God's character have been stressed—His holiness, His righteousness, and His sovereignty, for example. Today the focus of many religious people is on His love. No doubt many could echo Robert Browning's statement in *Paracelsus*, "God! Thou art love! I build my faith on that." However, the truth in this assertion is beclouded by current speculations about the love of God that are cultural rather than Biblical.

A Distorted Definition of Love

Apparently for some, God's love is really His indulgence or permissiveness and finds its unique expression in His forgiveness, with other aspects of His character (such as holiness or justice) not being taken seriously. From this perspective it would appear that love means letting me alone to do what I want and then comforting me if I get into difficulty. While it is true that God comforts and forgives, His love is to be understood in light of His character as revealed in the Bible. Yet it is interesting that one classic definition of God, found in the *Westminster Shorter Catechism*, fails to mention love but does name His wisdom, power, holiness, justice, goodness, and truth. Suffice it to say that we should affirm the vital significance of God's love as one of His attributes and should understand the Scriptural definition of His love to be found in both precept and illustration. Furthermore, we need to learn from Scripture the central place of love in the Christian's manner of life.

Dimensions of Love

To deal comprehensively with the subject of love as recorded in the Bible is not possible here, but some observations are in order.

Scripture abounds with examples of the believer's responsibility and privilege to meet both his neighbor's physical and temporal needs and to share the gospel with him. Such expressions of love must transcend racial, cultural, and economic barriers. In this brief consideration of the believer as an example in demonstrating love, I would like to elucidate a dimension of Biblical love almost universally overlooked or misunderstood. I submit that obeying both the First and Second Commandments and living out the Apostle John's teaching about love must be linked to our submission and response to our Lord's chastening of us as His children. This same kind of love in us is manifested as we care enough to confront and desire the growth for a brother or sister that we seek for ourselves. Such love finds appropriate expression, therefore, both in obedience to God and in ministry to His people.

The word for *love* we are considering (*agape*) can be translated "truly love" and is found in more than one hundred verses of the New Testament, and more than once in some of those verses. These references illuminate for us this aspect of the character of God. Then, too, from these passages we can better understand the meaning of the commandment to love God. In addition, studying a few of these verses will help us gain insight about expressing the full dimension of this love.

Love is first and foremost a characteristic of God. When Scripture in Genesis 1:26 says, "Let *us* make man in *our* image," it suggests the Trinity, or *a divine plurality in unity*. This doctrine sheds light on the expression, "God is love" (1 John 4:8). Because God existed before the universe came into being and before people were created, it follows that love was present in eternity past, even when nothing else was present. Let me explain.

If love requires an object to be truly love, what was there to be loved before the world existed? I believe the answer is, the members of the Trinity loved one another. Thus in the very being of the Triune God are found the subjects and the objects of love—one loving the other. The Father loved the Son and the Holy Spirit; the Son loved the Father and the Holy Spirit; the Holy Spirit loved the Father and the Son. This interaction in the very being of God is simply stated: "God is love." Such love did not have to wait until the creation of mankind to find its proper expression; it is inherent within the very nature and being of God Himself. Thus the Godhead characterizes "truly love," defines it, exemplifies it, and then demands it.

The Bible emphasizes that God's love for us is not dependent on our response but is *unconditional*. One of the most familiar verses in all of the Scriptures declares that "God so loved the world that he gave his one and only Son" (John 3:16). The Apostle Paul spoke of this as well: "But God demonstrates his own love for us in this: While we were still sinners, Christ died for us" (Romans 5:8). Manifestly, the redemptive love of God is not conditioned by the sinner's response, but rather continues to be available today in the gospel despite widespread indifference and rejection.

God's love is also unconditional as far as His continuing relationship to His people is concerned. An illustration of such love can be seen in the Parable of the Prodigal Son (Luke 15:11-32). Even though this young man had squandered his wealth in wild living, he was welcomed when he returned to his father's house. If God's love for us were dependent on our behavior as Christians, the fickleness of it would be more like our love than His. How grateful every Christian should be for the constancy of His Heavenly Father's love!

Love Manifested in Chastening

Not only is the love of God unconditional, accepting, and forgiving, but Scripture reveals God's love as also purposeful. At this point the Biblical description of God's love runs counter to modern conceptions that indicate, "He is always ready to forgive" and stop there. The Word of God in Hebrews is unequivocal in declaring:

My son, do not make light of the Lord's discipline, and do not lose heart when he rebukes you, because the Lord disciplines those he loves, and he punishes everyone he accepts as a son. (12:5, 6)

That God's chastening of us manifests His love is a remarkable assertion. Yet this passage emphasizes that one of the visible signs of our redemption and relationship to God is that we are chastened by Him. Moreover, this chastening is not necessarily because of disobedience. When Jesus was asked the question, "Rabbi, who sinned, this man or his parents, that he was born blind?," our Lord's reply was, "Neither this man nor his parents sinned, but this happened so that the work of God might be displayed in his life" (John 9:2, 3). Similarly, the chastening ministry of God in the life of the believer is not only because of misdeeds but also for the purposeful development of the individual.

No discipline seems pleasant at the time, but painful. Later on, however, it produces a harvest of righteousness and peace for those who have been trained by it. (Hebrews 12:11)

Even more remarkable is the Biblical teaching that God's only begotten Son was subjected to purposeful discipline:

Although he was a son, he learned obedience from what he suffered and, once made perfect, he became the source of eternal salvation for all who obey him. . . . (Hebrews 5:8)

When we complain that the Lord must not love us when He chastens us, we overlook the sublime example provided us in the action of the Heavenly Father toward His only begotten Son. We are certain that the Father loved the Son. Equally certain is the fact that God "laid on him the iniquity of us all" (Isaiah 53:6), for in the Garden our Savior groaned, "Father, if you are willing, take this cup from me . . ." (Luke 22:42). Recall, too, the unique situation of Christ on the cross as He cried out, "My God, my God, why have you forsaken me?" (Matthew 27:46). In some mysterious way, the sinless Son of God learned obedience by the things which He suffered and, being made complete, became the author of salvation to as many as obey Him.

Scripture is replete with examples of those who matured through chastening. Job, a man who was careful to do the will of God and yet suffered severely, learned much through his chastening experience. The necessity of a new perspective on his relationship to God caused Job to confess, "I despise myself and repent in dust and ashes" (42:6).

Early in his life Joseph learned of the purposes of God for him. Yet for years he was despised by his brothers, then cast into prison, where he was forgotten by a man he helped. Still he continued faithful until the time God honored him, and thus he was able to say to his brothers, "You intended to harm me, but God intended it for good . . ." (Genesis 50:20).

David, described as a man after God's own heart (1 Samuel 13:14), was beset with difficulty from the time he was anointed to be king. He was subjected to persecutions before he took office and troubles and heartaches after he was crowned. Yet throughout David's life the chastening love of God resulted in spiritual growth and blessing.

The Apostle Paul certainly experienced both God's love and His testing. In retrospect Paul could say, ". . . we also rejoice in our sufferings, because we know that suffering produces perseverance; perseverance, character; and character, hope. And hope does not disappoint us, because God has poured out his love into our hearts by the Holy Spirit, whom he has given us" (Romans 5:3-5). In reflecting on his own life, Paul remarked, ". . . I will boast all the more gladly about my weaknesses, so that Christ's power may rest on me" (2 Corinthians 12:9).

Consider also the great heroes of the faith listed or referred to in

Hebrews 11, many of whom endured dreadful circumstances and yet are not even named. The Scriptures say of them, "All these people were still living by faith when they died. They did not receive the things promised; they only saw them and welcomed them from a distance" (v. 13). During the long centuries of the church's history some individuals have experienced terrible suffering, often culminating in the loss of their lives. They died in faith, believing that the inscrutable purposes of God would be worked out, even though for them there was never the completeness of blessing that characterized the lives of others such as Job, Joseph, David, or the Apostle Paul.

Love Yields Obedience

In light of these challenging accounts from the Scriptures, we should ponder and then appreciate the words of our Lord in John 14, particularly verses 21 and 23:

> Whoever has my commands and obeys them, he is the one who loves me. He who loves me will be loved by my Father, and I too will love him and show myself to him. . . . If anyone loves me, he will obey my teaching. My Father will love him, and we will come to him and make our home with him.

Our Lord's emphasis here is that love and obedience are, so to speak, organically connected. Thus none of us can say truly that we love the Lord if we are being disobedient to what He commands. As God's purposeful love is made manifest in our hearts and lives, our understanding and reception of it cannot simply be abstract but must be expressed in obedient action.

As we have seen, Jesus Himself confessed that He loved the Father and that the Father loved Him. The demonstration of this was that He always did those things which pleased His Heavenly Father (John 5:30). Similarly, our only authentic response to God's love is unconditional obedience. "If anyone comes to me and does not hate

his father and mother, his wife and children, his brothers and sisters—
yes, even his own life—he cannot be my disciple" (Luke 14:26). Until
we manifest this kind of response, our discipleship is inadequate and
incomplete.

Scripture portrays the Lord Jesus looking on a rich young ruler
and loving him, then giving him a seemingly harsh stipulation: "If you
want to be perfect, go, sell your possessions and give to the poor, and
you will have treasure in heaven. Then come, follow me" (Matthew
19:21). The major issue here was not wealth. Rather, it was the question whether anything was competing for the young man's allegiance
and was thus inhibiting his submission to Christ's sovereignty over his
life.

This incident helps us understand that Christ's purposeful love is
incredibly and totally demanding. It requires of us all that we are and
have. C. S. Lewis, in *The Problem of Pain*, strikingly describes God
as "the consuming fire Himself, the Love that made the worlds, persistent as the artist's love for his work and despotic as a man's love
for a dog, jealous, inexorable, exacting as love between the sexes." It
was painful for the rich young ruler to learn that following Jesus
involved a total response to such a love.

Perspective Clarified Through Discipline

Having considered these Biblical insights into the correlation between
divine love and discipline, we need now to understand something
about the harvest of righteousness and peace promised to those who
have learned from God's training through discipline. An important
aspect of this is a realistic perspective which focuses our love where
it should be. The Word of God puts it this way:

> Do not love the world or anything in the world. If anyone loves
> the world, the love of the Father is not in him. For everything
> in the world—the cravings of sinful man, the lust of his eyes and

the boasting of what he has and does—comes not from the Father but from the world. (1 John 2:15, 16)

Such a perspective helps us avoid costly experiences which underscore the obvious fact that love for God and love for the world cannot coexist. We must recognize also that at work in the Christian's life is a principle of displacement; i.e., it is not possible to fill one's life both with love for God and love for the corruption, lustfulness, pride, and self-seeking that are characteristic of this age. The two are mutually incompatible. We must choose (see Joshua 24:15)!

If we really understand God's love and the response He expects of us, we know He will tolerate no rival claims on our allegiance. He must be sovereign in our hearts and lives if we are to enjoy a meaningful relationship with Him.

Correcting a Fellow Believer

The Christian who is an example for the believer in love must of necessity demonstrate God's unconditional but purposeful and exacting love as he deals with his fellow Christians. If we love one another, we can anticipate occasions when loving action may hurt, and yet it will be for the good of the other person. As is true of God's loving chastening of us, correction from a fellow believer will better enable the individual receiving this to be a partaker of God's holiness and to evidence the peaceable fruit of righteousness.

Despite the Biblical encouragement to manifest the kind of brotherly love that corrects, we too often presume it is more loving to pass by on the other side, to ignore what is going on. Occasionally I find that someone in the fellowship of which I am a part is not living as he should. When I ask whether others know about the undesirable activity, I find that they do. When I inquire why no one went to the person in question to raise the issue, I receive the reply, "That's his business." Such response cannot be Christian love, even though some might say it is loving not to disturb or challenge another believer or to make him uncomfortable.

Scripture teaches that love does not shirk its responsibilities. Consider the illustration in the second chapter of Galatians, when in confronting Peter, his compromising brother in Christ, Paul "opposed him to his face, because he was clearly in the wrong" (v. 11). This act exhibited brotherly love on Paul's part—to save Peter from himself.

If there are those under our direction who are doing things that are not right, we must not consider it loving to condone their actions out of fear of being intruders. Rather, "watch yourself, or you also may be tempted" (Galatians 6:1), and then seek in humility to restore such a one.

Once when I was in real difficulty and seemed unable to cope with a problem, some brothers in Christ visited me. These men assured me that because they loved me, they thought it necessary to rebuke me. So they did. Ever since, I have been grateful to them because only when they ministered to me in this confrontational way was I able to face the problem and deal with it.

What moved me deeply was their attitude. Obviously it was painful for them to come to me. They were suffering distinct emotional stress. Yet in Christian love they refused to dismiss the matter as my personal business. Instead they sought, in humility and with sensitivity, to be the spiritual ones who restored another in a spirit of meekness as an expression of their Christian love (Galatians 6:1).

What these friends did was in the spirit of an important but often overlooked incident in the incarnate ministry of our Lord. This is found in the account of Jesus' washing His disciples' feet (John 13:1-17). Both His action and His accompanying instruction provide important emphases to guide us as we seek, so to speak, to wash one another's feet and so follow His example.

Clearly our Lord did something which in the culture of His day was incongruous. A recognized leader simply did not take the role, even briefly, of a slave. Yet Jesus did so without in any way abdicating His position. The text is clear. He affirmed His position as Lord and Master and Teacher, yet functioned as a servant. He had not forgotten His relationship to God the Father, or the mission and motive of His ministry. He knew He had come from God and was going to God, and He was committed to loving His own to the uttermost—as the cross would soon demonstrate.

His act of washing His disciples' feet, particularly Peter's, and His explanation and command to follow His example, furnish us with important insights regarding humble, purposeful love and service. First of all, as He explained to Peter, the example He set did not relate to that comprehensive cleansing which takes place when an individual as a sinner comes to Christ in repentance and faith and is forgiven of all his sin. The example of washing we are to follow deals, rather, with daily defilement. Here the ministry of a fellow believer is crucial.

However, the objective is not only to bring about cleansing from the uncleanness we pick up in our walk in this world. As Jesus said to Peter, the act is also one of identity with Christ ("Unless I wash you, you have no part with me," v. 8).

Hence, our ministry to others in the Body of Christ is because we know who we are (His disciples) and what our ministry is (to promote the peace, purity, and edification of the Lord's people). As leaders we do not abdicate our positions any more than Jesus did, for He reminded His disciples that He washed their feet as their Lord and Teacher. In the security of our identity and our calling, we too are free to serve. Then we encourage repentance and correction, but we do so to emphasize identification with those committed to the Lordship of Christ and indeed to Christ Himself. Disobedience not only alienates, but also obscures our relationship to our sovereign Lord.

The case of church discipline recounted in 1 Corinthians 5 illustrates this. The erring brother needed not only to repent but also to be restored to fellowship. His repudiation of his sin—prompted by the corrective action of the church leadership—readied him for their reception of him once again. Thus their ministry incorporated both purification and identification.

In undertaking a ministry of correction, however, we must keep in mind another important aspect of our Lord's example. The disciples knew from sustained and intimate contact with Him that He was faithful to the will and the work of the Father. Thus they were ready, even eager, to receive His ministry. When we are scrupulous to deal with sin in our own lives and are committed to obedience as a way of life, *then* we are in a position to minister to others. Also, while our Lord did not need others to minister to Him in this way, we should welcome those who minister to us. Clearly the outcome is that we may continue to be fit to lead by serving and to "wash" because we ourselves are those washed and identified with our Lord and Teacher.

In the home, too, as well as in the Christian community generally, children who are disciplined often appreciate the love that expresses itself through purposeful guidance and correction. Even in Christian higher education I have encountered young people who have had no shortage of money, experience, and opportunity and yet had a profound inner emptiness. In virtually every case a major factor was a lack of parental love and discipline. The parents had provided lavishly for everything but what their children needed most. Too often this defective parental awareness results in tragic consequences.

One is reminded of the loving sternness Anne Sullivan used in dealing with Helen Keller again and again. The six-year-old Helen had become almost ungovernable. Finally in a dramatic encounter at the dinner table, Helen pounded on the table and created a scene. Despite the objections of Helen's father, Miss Sullivan took the child outside and forced her to come to terms with her teacher. As she and Helen stood by the pump in the yard, the little girl reached out her hand and felt the water, then succeeded for the first time in forming the word "water." She finally understood!

The father suddenly intervened and took Helen back inside. Miss

Sullivan despaired that she had lost the child. Yet in one of the most poignant incidents of the entire experience, Helen returned to Miss Sullivan, reached up to touch her face, identified it as that of her teacher, and very gently kissed her on the cheek.

Did Miss Sullivan love the child? Without question she did. Thankfully, little Helen came to realize that her teacher's stern discipline was an evidence of purposeful love so that the child might develop a capability to learn. In this way her teacher manifested love that was akin to the love of God—a love that was not permissive but highly directive, that when necessary was strict but was always for the ultimate good of the child. Furthermore, from all that we can ascertain, Miss Sullivan was careful to distinguish between discipline and abuse, between that which was constructive and that which was destructive.

The Rewards of Obedience

Obedience, then, is a critical component in the full expression of love. Love that is demonstrated in obedience to our Savior's commands produces a remarkable result, for we gain a depth and a comprehensiveness of understanding we did not have before and could have no other way. The experience of happily married persons illustrates this principle. They fell in love, as the saying goes, and were married. Then as their love deepened, they increasingly found wellsprings of understanding and insight in the other person that they had not seen at first.

When our Savior said, "If anyone loves me, he will obey my teaching" (John 14:23), he immediately connected these words with this statement: ". . . the Counselor, the Holy Spirit, whom the Father will send in my name, will teach you all things and will remind you of everything I have said to you" (v. 26). Thus our obedience to the Lord in keeping His commandments as an expression of our love for Him is linked to the disclosure of truth through the ministry of the Holy Spirit.

Similarly, there is a correlation between love and obedience and between obedience and disclosure in verses 21 and 23 of John 14. "Whoever has my commands and obeys them, he is the one who loves me. He who loves me will be loved by my Father, and I too will love him and show myself to him" (v. 21). Here the Savior promises to manifest Himself to those who in obedience express their love for Him. In a sense, by obedience we have validated our right to the Lord's special disclosure of Himself.

Verse 23 provides an additional illustration of the same concept. "If anyone loves me, he will obey my teaching. My Father will love him, and we will come to him and make our home with him." One way to come to know others better is to live in their homes. Very quickly you will discover facets of their personality and character you did not know before. People often wear a façade, but at home they will manifest their real selves. As God makes His home with us, we learn to know Him better and He becomes more and more intimately involved with our lives.

The disclosure discussed in this passage involves each of the Persons in the Trinity. If someone loves the Lord and keeps His commandments, God the Holy Spirit will teach him the truth, God the Son will manifest Himself to him, and both the Son and the Father will come and take up Their abode with him.

One of the marks of the believer, then, is an increasing awareness of the greatness and the glory of the Lord whom we serve. Inspired by this vision, our love will deepen and our obedience will be more effective, while the absence of this awareness will result in a barrenness that is the opposite of vibrant Christian living. Such living needs to be manifested in the world in which we live, particularly by those called to Christian leadership.

The love that commands, chastens, and molds contrasts starkly with the defective caricatures of the word all too common in the late twentieth century. The world, with its distorted view of the love of God, should be able to look to the believer for accurate definition and consistent exemplification. Christians must have compassion for a world dominated by self-seeking and perversions and must bear witness to a better way. Having comprehended and welcomed God's unconditional but purposeful and exacting love, they are privileged to demonstrate to the world the authenticity and practicality of Christian commitment.

7

Words

A leader must be able to communicate clearly. But leaders in our world face a problem related to the exercise of this capability. One of the paradoxes of our times is that never before has there been a greater torrent of words both written and spoken clamoring for our attention, and never has there been a more profound sense of mistrust of what we read and hear. Listeners to some public figures, for example, routinely assume that what these speakers say should not be believed because their statements are only "for the record." The guiding principle of many leaders seems to be expediency rather than truth, and public opinion determines whether they should contradict or stand by what they have said.

We should not conclude, however, that today's public servants are necessarily more untruthful than those of previous generations. Our heightened awareness of their inconsistency arises from the fact that now we have instant replay. Years ago a public figure might have successfully denied saying something because of a delay in reporting, a failure to record what was said, or a misunderstanding on the part of the reporter. But today a technician presses a button and in living color the official is portrayed repeating exactly what he might otherwise be tempted to deny he had said.

Unfortunately, the credibility gap cannot be limited to any one group. Whether there be distrust of the pronouncements of a head of government or of the statements of employees calling in "sick," everyone is assumed to know "the rules of the game." The double *entendre* applies today to more than suggestive jokes. Yet most people have at least some sense of the wrongness of dishonest, misleading speech and of the appropriateness of being well-informed.

Despite the atmosphere of distrust about verbal communication, we continue to have a daily newspaper circulation of many millions. Thousands of book titles are published each year, in addition to thousands of new editions. Consider also that the law of contract remains an indispensable part of our economic and social life. Giving our word, despite the abuse of trust in this age, is still an essential expectation.

"And God Said . . ."

Within the Christian community the importance of words can scarcely be overestimated. The leader who desires to speak honestly and effectively does well to review the Scriptural precedent for clear and godly communication. Repeatedly the Bible describes God's communication with man in the simple phrase, "and God said." He did not choose to convey His revelation differently to each individual or through unrecorded events and encounters; rather, in the Scriptures He verbalized His message to everyone.

Furthermore, the proclamation of the Good News is necessary to fulfill the Great Commission (Matthew 28:19, 20), and man's response involves a stated confession of Jesus Christ as Savior and Lord (Romans 10:9, 10). Even in eternity verbal exclamations of praise will abound. (Consider, for example, Revelation 4, 5.)

Some individuals, however, argue that acts of mercy, helpfulness, and concern are more important than statements which declare the Biblical message of the gospel. During a meeting some years ago a professor commented that Jesus never talked about His faith but simply went about doing good. In response, I asked when he had last read the New Testament. He admitted that he had not done so recently. I suggested that consulting the New Testament, the most creditable record we have about Jesus, would provide evidence that He not only did good deeds, but also spoke at length to the people to declare His message to them.

By placing obvious emphasis on words, Jesus validated the assumption that the significance of words is compatible with both the nature of God and the nature of man. To be sure, some might say that the metaphysical union of Father, Son, and Holy Spirit does not require verbalized communication. In their integral relationship, the members of the Trinity might seem not to need to speak to one another. But we have Scriptural evidence to the contrary. For example, consider this quotation: "Then God said, 'Let us make man in our image, in our likeness, and let them rule over the fish of the sea and the birds of the air . . .'" (Genesis 1:26).

Scripture here portrays the Trinity engaged in conversation. Similarly, Genesis 11:7 reads, "Come, let us go down and confuse their language. . . ." We may infer that the Father was speaking to the Son and to the Holy Spirit. Although all three Persons in the Trinity are equal in power and glory, in a functional sense God the Father exercises sovereign oversight. Thus we can conclude that He was speaking on these occasions, using words to communicate with the Son and with the Holy Spirit.

Consider also that when our Lord Jesus Christ came to earth, He was called "the Word," a term connoting reasoned discourse. This tells us something very significant about the nature of God's revelation. It was disclosed generally in what Jesus Christ did, to be sure, but specifically in what He said. His earthly ministry, therefore, confirmed that by divinely inspired discourse a personal God chose to reveal Himself to man.

Similarly, the Holy Spirit ministers explicitly through words. Such ministry made possible the verbal inspiration of Scripture, as well as man's understanding of Biblical truth. The Apostle Paul, in a key statement in 1 Corinthians 2, explains that while sinful human beings understand one another because they have the same spirit, they cannot comprehend the things of God because they lack the illumination of the Holy Spirit.

> The man without the Spirit does not accept the things that come from the Spirit of God, for they are foolishness to him, and he cannot understand them, because they are spiritually discerned. (v. 14)

And in this same context the apostle emphasizes:

> This is what we speak, not in words taught us by human wisdom but in words taught by the Spirit, expressing spiritual truths in spiritual words. (v. 13)

Within the limits of individual personality and style, the Spirit moved upon the writers of Scripture to enable them to choose the words needed to transmit God's truth. Furthermore, the Holy Spirit enables earnest readers to understand these words and thus to grasp God's truth verbally conveyed. Thus we who are convinced that God has revealed truth propositionally (i.e., in words) differ from others in the religious community who argue that meaning can be gained only by experience or by encounter.

Words Are Integral to Witness

Words are essential not only for a full understanding of God's truth, but also for an adequate response to that truth. As we have observed, words are vital to our coming to God through Jesus Christ. Romans 10:9, 10 specifies that while with the heart we believe unto righteousness, it is with the mouth that confession is made unto salvation. Further, Scripture teaches us that we make this confession because of the ministry of the Holy Spirit (1 John 4:2); it is He who enables us to confess Jesus Christ as Lord. The Trinity works in concert, then, to ensure our salvation.

After having received Christ as Savior and confessing Him as Lord, we are enabled by the Spirit to overcome to a significant degree the problem of communication that became so severe at the Tower of Babel. In contrast to that confusion, coherence was made possible by the Holy Spirit at Pentecost and afterward. This capability is implicit in the Biblical promise that describes our witness:

> "But you will receive power when the Holy Spirit comes on you;
> and you will be my witnesses. . . ." (Acts 1:8)

Words Flow from Thoughts

We use words to communicate, and care is to be exercised in all our speech, so that we do not contradict God's truth or sully our witness to His name. Let me illustrate.

While serving in the Navy in a combat zone, I discovered that a young ensign had moved a gun crew from their stations to work elsewhere aboard ship. Consequently, these men—part of my division—had left the anti-aircraft battery unmanned, a clear violation of standing orders. I was furious and can yet remember calling the ensign to the control station and publicly using profanity to describe him as a certain kind of fool.

Instantly I realized that I had cursed this young man. I went back to my room discouraged with myself. I had been conducting a Bible class and in other ways had endeavored to witness for the Lord. How could I, a Christian, have acted in this way?

I then realized that because I was hearing profanity day after day, I would think these expressions when I became provoked. Then in this instance I myself swore because my inhibitions were overcome by my anger. What had been in my mind inevitably came out in my words.

But this applies to more than profanity. If we harbor jealousy, bitterness, or hatred, such attitudes will inevitably find expression.

Sadly, we misunderstand our problem if we succeed in not using profane words and yet make comments that are sarcastic or belittling or are deliberately calculated to embarrass another. For example, some husbands seem to gain a perverse pleasure from publicly ridiculing their wives ("Just like a woman!"). I have observed that the wife may join in the laughter, but the experience is nevertheless humiliating and contributes to her poor self-image—and damages the marriage relationship as well.

Similarly, to brand a subordinate as stupid or a fool may well put us in the vulnerable position of being found guilty of denigrating the crown of God's creative activity—a man or woman made in His image. Whatever our Savior's sober warning in Matthew 5:22 means ("But anyone who says, 'You fool!' will be in danger of the fire of hell"), it is at least a strong inhibition against castigating another individual in this way.

Scripture has some important emphases about this kind of hurtful speech. In Romans 3:14 "cursing" and "bitterness" describe the behavior pattern of those who have turned away from God (vv. 11, 12). Also, the Apostle Paul in Ephesians 4:31 links "bitterness, rage and anger" with "brawling," "slander," and "malice" and indicates these are all grievous to the indwelling Holy Spirit, whom we are commanded not to sadden (v. 30). God desires our obedience on this point. Surely we should be able to obey a command as well as give one, for every leader is both a superior (over other people) and a subordinate (to our Lord and Master).

Further, the writer of Hebrews urges Christians to "See to it that no bitter root grows up to cause trouble and defile many" (12:15). It is awesome to realize that a leader's potential to affect others negatively is far greater than that of a subordinate, and thus he must bear the greater responsibility for the defilement caused by destructive comments.

Of concern also is the misuse of words by lifting them out of context or manipulating them to fit a preconceived objective. Surely we would not want to be identified with the methods recorded in Matthew 26:59-62, when false evidence was solicited against Jesus and "many false witnesses came forward." We also should not be superficial in our appraisal, as the disciples were when they permitted their provincialism to affect their perception of a man (not associated with the Twelve) who was casting out demons in the Lord's name (Luke 9:49).

Remember also that in 2 Corinthians 12:20 "gossip" is grouped with such things as "anger," "slander," "arrogance" and "disorder"—all of which are to be avoided.

The words of Jesus recorded in the Gospel of Matthew document my assertion, drawn from my shipboard experience, that we speak what is in our hearts:

". . . out of the overflow of the heart the mouth speaks. The good man brings good things out of the good stored up in him, and the evil man brings evil things out of the evil stored up in him." (12:34, 35)

When the Savior declared that from the abundance of the heart the mouth speaks, He was affirming that the total personality is thus revealed.

Romans 10 provides an excellent summary of the Scriptural ramifications of the word *heart*. The heart has desires or emotions (v. 1), is capable of speculative thought (v. 6), and can believe (vv. 9, 10).

A Biblical illustration of the overflow of the heart can be found in the account of the surplus of food gathered after the feeding of the four thousand (Mark 8:1-10). Such an outpouring or surplus of the heart discloses the real person.

When I was president of Wheaton College, I learned that a brief interview with a potential candidate for appointment to a position was not adequate. Candidates usually arrived sartorially perfect and with their responses carefully rehearsed. Sometimes they appeared to have read books on interviews and were following a recommended pattern of behavior. Having read some of the same books, I found the process amusing.

But I was not getting accurate impressions of the candidates. It was all too formal and structured to permit them to be themselves. So I asked that each applicant be with us for several hours, preferably overnight. After some time had passed, the candidate would relax and talk freely. Then I would learn more about the real person. From uninhibited conversation I gained insights previously obscured.

God's Word Penetrates

If it is agreed that inner attitudes influence actions, what constructive action may be taken to deal with our subjective selves? I suggest we must permit the Word of God to influence our inner being. The words of God can both judge and correct the believer. The writer of Hebrews contends that God's Word probes into the personal and private aspects of our lives. This somewhat enigmatic teaching indicates that no sanctuary, either physical or metaphysical, exists into which the Word of God cannot penetrate and then pass judgment.

> The word of God is living and active. Sharper than any double-edged sword, it penetrates even to dividing soul and spirit, joints and marrow; it judges the thoughts and attitudes of the heart. (4:12)

What sensitive and informed Christian has not been struck with the judgmental quality of Holy Scripture as the Spirit of God has used the Word of God to speak to a particular circumstance or action or attitude? God's statements to us in His Word, therefore, both provide conviction for wrongdoing and validation for that which is consistent with the will of God. The words of God in Scripture judge the individual, and the words of the individual are subject to God's judgment.

Many of the sins Paul lists as indicative of "the old man" who is to be put off for a new life in Christ concern one's use of words.

> . . . each of you must put off falsehood and speak truthfully to his neighbor. . . . "In your anger do not sin." . . . Do not let any unwholesome talk come out of your mouths. . . . Get rid of all bitterness, rage and anger. . . . (Ephesians 4:25-32)

Avoiding outbursts of inappropriate speech requires constant attention and mental discipline. Once, when I was under unrelenting pressure, a dear friend came to say hello. Though I responded to his greeting, I am sure I conveyed to him, "What do you mean interrupting my schedule when I don't have any time to see you?"

Afterward I felt obliged to write to that colleague and apologize. I had failed to recognize that I was getting too frustrated and tense and thus was vulnerable to the kind of reaction that hurt my friend. I needed to ask the Lord for grace and strength and also the determination to make corrections in my schedule. Too often we destroy in an instant what took months or years to develop because of the condition of our hearts that finds expression in our mouths and demonstration in our actions.

The fact that our uninhibited speech reveals what we really are should be cause for realistic self-examination and then corrective action. We cannot presume that being in a position of Christian leadership guarantees a consistent right use of the tongue. On occasion I have been disillusioned to hear Christian leaders relate anecdotes of questionable taste. I have also heard some leaders use humor at the expense of another. When I observe an individual habitually depreciating others and telling jokes at their expense, I ask myself what motivates such talk. Often such hostility against others springs from a leader's sense of inadequacy or insecurity.

Far too often the speech of even those in leadership positions suggests a serious character problem. Perhaps incidents of a sensitive and personal nature are shared in a manner that can only be described as gossip. Or maybe something reported as fact is unsubstantiated or questionable.

Perhaps even more serious is a selective and faulty use of Scripture to justify our prejudices or to support our jaundiced view of another believer. Such manipulation of the Word of God is not only faulty exegesis but an abdication of our responsibility to declare divine revelation accurately for the glory of God. To use the Bible as a weapon to indulge personal spite or antipathy dishonors both the written Word and the living Word and grieves the blessed Holy Spirit.

When the Scriptures maintain, therefore, that "men will have to give account on the day of judgment for every careless word they have spoken" (Matthew 12:36), it is clear that our words must constantly be submitted to our Lord's leadership. Our careless or idle words are uninhibited words, words that accurately reveal our inner condition. When our speech reflects a spiritually oriented heart, we can confidently expect the blessing of God; when it does not, we can be sure of His chastening. To secure the blessing and avoid the judgment, we must be diligent in our obedience to the Word of God and in our openness to the Holy Spirit. Furthermore, the authenticity of our witness ought to merit not only the blessing of God but also the approbation of men. This kind of witness commends the Christian message to those who have judged other pronouncements and found them wanting.

These factors should combine to motivate us to fulfill our Lord's command to be His witnesses and so merit His "Well done" in that day when our words as well as our deeds will be judged by God.

As Christian leaders, therefore, let us take time to cultivate our inner being through prayer and meditation upon God's Word and through the appropriation of the fullness of the Holy Spirit. By our words we will be justified as the Holy Spirit inspires and enables us to manifest His fruit in the way we speak.

8

Faith

*Now faith is being sure of what we hope for and certain of
what we do not see. This is what the ancients were commended for. By faith we understand that the universe was
formed at God's command, so that what is seen was not
made out of what was visible. By faith Abel offered God a
better sacrifice than Cain did. By faith he was commended
as a righteous man, when God spoke well of his offerings.
And by faith he still speaks, even though he is dead. By faith
Enoch was taken from this life, so that he did not experience death; he could not be found, because God had taken
him away. For before he was taken, he was commended as
one who pleased God. And without faith it is impossible to
please God, because anyone who comes to him must believe
that he exists and that he rewards those who earnestly seek
him.* (Hebrews 11:1-6)

This passage beautifully and accurately defines *faith*, contrasting it sharply with the "seeing is believing" philosophy all too
common even among Christian leaders.

Some years ago I was in a meeting of a group of believers who
had been involved in calling a new leader for their organization. Their

chairman showed us an unopened airmail special delivery letter from the candidate we had invited to fill the position. Before opening the letter, he asked the group to pray that they might accept whatever the contents would reveal. So everyone prayed. Then the chairman dramatically opened the letter, read it, and excitedly told us the man had accepted the job. We all rejoiced. God had graciously met our expectations. It was an inspiring moment.

Months later I asked the man who had been chosen about his letter of acceptance. Quite casually he remarked that earlier in the day on which the letter was received, he had called our chairman and told him he was coming. I was disillusioned. The incident had been manufactured, with the supposed justification that we needed to have our faith buttressed by a contrivance.

Nothing in the Biblical record supports such a deceitful approach. Instead, Scripture provides outstanding illustrations of the integrity and other qualities that ought to characterize Christian leaders. Trusting completely in a faithful God is one such attribute. Even if a Christian's professional future is at stake or if his relationships with other people are an issue, he must first of all be obedient to the commandments and purposes of God. He must trust the sovereign Lord to work out all things after the counsel of His own will. Manipulating others, even to strengthen their faith, has no part in Christian ministry.

Before citing certain individuals as examples of faith in action, Hebrew 11 begins with a short definition of faith: "being sure of what we hope for and certain of what we do not see." The passage goes on to suggest why faith is vital to our relationship with God: "And without faith it is impossible to please God, because anyone who comes to him must believe that he exists and that he rewards those who earnestly seek him."

God Lives Now

First consider the latter part of that statement, which indicates that faith is incompatible with both atheism and deism. The former denies that God "exists," and the latter does not believe He will "reward those who earnestly seek him."

Those who come to God must believe He exists. The verb is in the present tense. God is *now* a living reality; He is not a historical curiosity. To have faith, one must hold this assumption or presupposition.

Furthermore, it is essential to Biblical faith that God be recognized as a personal Deity who may be approached directly by His people. Not all religionists accept this view.

A number of prominent individuals in the American Colonial and Revolutionary periods were deists. They believed in God but insisted He was so distant from man that it was not possible for human beings to be in personal contact with Him. They thought instead that whatever God wanted man to know could be seen in the natural creation and understood by reason.

In more modern times, some theologians have spoken of God as being so wholly other that, again, it is not possible to have any personal relationship with Him. As a consequence, man is essentially left to himself.

In contrast to such notions, Biblical faith presumes that God exists today and is responsive to those who diligently seek Him. Our Lord Jesus Christ affirmed this fact in the account recorded in Matthew 16:13-20. After Peter had made his great confession that Jesus was "the Christ, the Son of the living God," Jesus announced that flesh and blood had not revealed this concept to him; the Father in Heaven had disclosed it. God the Father had given Peter the insight that the Man standing before him was Christ, the Son of the living God.

Here we learn not only about the person of Christ but also about the nature of God and His communication with man. In fact, when our Savior said that flesh and blood did not reveal those truths to Peter, he meant that this knowledge came not by report nor by observation nor by human speculation, but by the revelation of God.

Faith, then, presumes that God communicates with man. Faith also presumes that God responds to His people. James Hudson Taylor is quoted as saying that what is important is not so much that we have faith, but that our faith is in a faithful God. We believe in a God who is able to do "immeasurably more than all we ask or imagine" (Ephesians 3:20). Faith is important primarily because of the character of God.

Faith Understands Creation

In the Hebrews passage we find also an indication of the comprehensive significance of faith. Referring to the past, Scripture says, "By faith we understand that the universe was formed at God's command, so that what is seen was not made out of what was visible" (v. 3). By faith we know that the creation, as theologians say, was made *ex nihilo*, out of nothing. God did not take previously existing material and form it into land and water. Matter is not eternal. Only God is eternal, and it was He who made the universe out of nothing. In fact, Scripture states, "He spoke, and it came to be" (see Psalm 33:6-9).

What a dramatic time that must have been! Imagine God saying, "Be created" and the universe coming into being. That would have been something to see! But the writer of Hebrews explains that faith is the only satisfactory way of knowing how it all began. It is by faith that we accept the fact that God spoke and it was done.

Faith Governs the Present

Hebrews 11 also makes mention of faith as a governing principle in the life of the believing community. The specific reference is to Abel, who was commended as a righteous man because he offered a better sacrifice than his brother (v. 4). In studying Abel's response, we may infer that faith is a working principle which can inform the life of the devout believer. Because Abel was sensitive to God, he made his offering by faith. In killing an animal from his flock, Abel demonstrated his belief that the sacrifice would be significant in God's sight. Thus Abel lived by faith and is a model to us in the present day.

Faith Brings Hope

Hebrews 11 also relates faith to the future. "By faith Enoch was taken from this life, so that he did not experience death . . ." (v. 5). Here we may conclude that faith in God and belief in eternal life are interrelated. With the poet the Christian can say:

> *Life is real! Life is earnest!*
> *And the grave is not its goal.*
> *"Dust thou art, to dust returnest,"*
> *Was not spoken of the soul."*
> (Henry Wadsworth Longfellow)

To summarize: By the Holy Spirit the writer of Hebrews gives us an insight into what constitutes faith—"being sure of what we hope for and certain of what we do not see." Faith is rooted in the character of a self-existent and self-revealing God. Faith is the key to understanding the past, living responsibly in the present, and possessing hope for the future. Therefore, faith comprehensively relates to the whole of life and has as its object a faithful God.

The Man of Faith

Of all Biblical examples of persons of faith, Abraham is best known. Scripture describes him this way:

By faith Abraham, when called to go to a place he would later receive as his inheritance, obeyed and went, even though he did not know where he was going. By faith he made his home in the promised land like a stranger in a foreign country. . . .
By faith Abraham, even though he was past age—and Sarah herself was barren—was enabled to become a father

because he considered him faithful who had made the promise. (Hebrews 11:8-11)

In considering Abraham as an illustration of the man of faith, we should note two major emphases: Abraham's exercise of faith in dealing with material things, and his exercise of faith in dealing with other persons. These provide splendid instances in which he acted in accordance with God's promises to him.

In Genesis 12 we read that the Lord told Abraham:

"Leave your country, your people and your father's household and go to the land I will show you. I will make you into a great nation and I will bless you; I will make your name great, and you will be a blessing. I will bless those who bless you, and whoever curses you I will curse; and all peoples on earth will be blessed through you." (vv. 1-3)

Abraham obeyed this command and went out, not knowing where he was going. And God honored Abraham because of his faith. In fact, when he came into the land, there the Lord added to what He had originally declared to Abraham: "To your offspring I will give *this* land" (Genesis 12:7).

Test, Pass, Test Again

At this point Abraham was put to the test, something that happens periodically in the walk of faith. A commandment (a test of obedience) is obeyed by faith—God gives more light—faith is tested.

The faith of Abraham was challenged when a disagreement developed between Lot's herdsmen and his own (Genesis 13:1-9). He was faced with a dilemma. Although God had promised Abraham this land, his herdsmen and those of his nephew could not get along. So Abraham had two alternatives: to tell Lot to get out, or to let Lot choose what he wanted.

As a man of faith, Abraham was willing to allow Lot to choose because he trusted God to honor His promise to give him the land. Whether or not Lot chose the land was not of major consequence. The promise was still there. When Abraham had passed the test of faith, *then* the Lord gave him this reassurance: "Lift up your eyes from where you are and look north and south, east and west. All the land that you see I will give to you and your offspring forever" (Genesis 13:14, 15).

The Lord had tested Abraham by asking, so to speak, "Do you really believe My promise?" When Abraham showed that he did indeed trust in God's sovereign power by letting Lot choose, then the Lord commended Abraham and promised to give him all that he could see. We conclude from this example that to have faith one must believe in the promise of God to such a degree that the intermediate maneuverings and changes will make no difference in his confidence about the ultimate purposes of God.

The writer of Hebrews recognized this principle in the lives of God's people of previous eras and chronicled their inspiring example of fidelity and trust despite alienation and persecution (11:13).

Evidencing faith when a favorable outcome cannot be humanly anticipated can prove to be very challenging. Some years ago I was ministering at a weekend retreat. Toward the end of our time together one of the group asked if he could talk privately with me. He was heavily in debt and had been manipulating his accounts so his creditors and the bank would not know of his problem. Finally his obligations became too heavy. He feared telling the truth to the bank personnel because he was sure they would call in his notes, and he would be bankrupt and disgraced. So he asked what he should do. How would he be able to continue to provide for his wife and children?

I encouraged the man to do the right thing, even though this would be difficult, and to trust God to take care of him afterward. By acting honestly he would honor God, and I was convinced God would not be unmindful of this obedience and trust.

The individual thanked me for my counsel, but he was still a miserable man. He was painfully aware that his affairs were in terrible disarray. I promised to pray for him. A few weeks later his wife wrote to tell me what had happened. One evening the whole family got on their knees in the living room and prayed that the Lord would give the husband/father the courage to do what he knew was right. Then he went to the bank and asked for an appointment with the president. He confessed that he had been deceiving the bank for many months and that he was now in a financial crisis.

After the fearful man had finished talking, the president of the bank told him he was willing to give him a chance because he believed that my friend would not have come to him had he not had something in his character that was worthy of confidence. They worked out a line of credit and a system whereby the man could pay his debts.

The following spring I saw a changed man. No longer did he have to manipulate his accounts or worry whether he would be found out. Instead, he obeyed God by being honest and forthright in his financial dealings. He was learning to count on the providence of God by faith.

We should be careful to note, however, that obeying God does not necessarily result in material benefits. God may have His own inscrutable reasons for withholding these tangible indications of His provision. Indeed, both from Scripture and from personal observation we know that this is the case. The account of the rich young ruler in Luke 18:18-30 underscores the fact that obedience to our sovereign Lord may result in substantial financial loss rather than gain. Whenever it would appear that material things are a deterrent to unconditional obedience to Christ our Lord, we should not be surprised if He expects renunciation in this area.

Further, the Scriptural dictum that "the love of money is a root of all kinds of evil" (1 Timothy 6:10) has its demonstration in more than the pagan world. Unfortunately, it may be seen within the precincts of organized Christendom. Some of the saddest chapters of church history attest to this, and the latent peril of preoccupation with the material and the economic is evident today as well.

It is regrettable that few Christians seem to be able to handle wealth responsibly. The preoccupation of the rich man and his brothers as recorded in Luke 16 has its counterpart today. Since God knows us so much better than we do ourselves, He may withhold that which He knows will detract from His glory and our good.

On the other hand, what we do in faith by obeying the Lord may sometimes produce surprising consequences. I once heard of a man who had been bribing a contractor because he understood this was the only way to get business from that firm. Even though the man was a Christian, he had paid the bribes over a period of three years.

Finally, his conscience so convicted him about this dishonest practice that he decided he would sin no more, contracts or no contracts. He went to the contractor's office and confessed that even though he had not acted like one, he was a Christian. He acknowledged that it was wrong to pay the bribes and said he would no longer continue the practice, even if he lost all the business from the firm.

To the man's surprise, the contractor began to weep and then told him he had been using the money from the bribes to finance a double life. Yet he had been hoping that somehow he could stop what he was doing and thanked the man for helping him change his behavior. Can you imagine what it did to the businessman to realize that in the midst of a system characterized by bribes and other under-the-counter dealings he could glorify God by resolving to believe and trust Him?

Faith Applies to Institutions

Living by faith can be representative of institutions as well as individuals. At Wheaton College we determined not to accept aid for current operations or capital improvements from the national or state government. A number of Christian colleges take such aid, and we recognize this is a matter for each college to decide. However, it is Wheaton College's conviction that the school should be as free as possible to be pervasively Christian in its programs and practices. So although Wheaton could divide its program into "sacred" and "secular" elements and receive aid for the secular parts, the school affirms that the life of the *entire* campus should be under the Lordship of Christ and the authority of Holy Scripture. This includes business affairs, advertising, athletics, and the integration of faith and learning in the classrooms. Foregoing hundreds of thousands of dollars that could be obtained from the national or state government for new construction or for operational grants-in-aid appears burdensome. Yet in extraordinary ways the college has experienced the validity of J. Hudson Taylor's statement: "God's work, done in God's way, will never lack God's supply."

Abraham Further Exemplifies Faith

Consider now some other illustrations from the life of Abraham that should encourage us to have confidence in God even when times of testing come. The trying of our faith may take a number of forms, as seen in the life of the patriarch. When Lot chose the better land, Abraham might well have felt that their relationship should come to an end. But he did not. In fact, when five kings overran Sodom and carried Lot away, Abraham defeated them and rescued Lot. Further, when the heavenly visitors told Abraham they were going to destroy Sodom, he interceded for his nephew and may very well have been instrumental in Lot's being spared (see Genesis 18:16-33).

Abraham, as a man of faith, trusted in God and was therefore at liberty to help his nephew, even though Lot was greedy for immediate gain. Secure in his faith, Abraham could still show love toward his nephew because he did not need to be concerned about what he was going to gain or lose.

Abraham's Failures to Trust God

We should remember, however, that in Egypt and at Gerar Abraham, giant of faith that he was, revealed that he did not always consistently live according to God's will. Abraham's problem lay in Sarah's beauty (Genesis 12:11ff.). In these incidents we have an example of the failure to apply the principle of faith at all times. Although God had met Abraham's needs for land and possessions, the patriarch still became fearful and unbelieving when personal relationships were involved. So he resorted to a contrivance. He called his wife his "sister" in the misguided hope that the local sovereign who might desire Sarah would spare his life as her "brother."

These experiences suggest an important truth to us. The exercise of faith is not like a diamond that keeps its quality forever, but like a skill that requires constant practice. Unless our faith becomes an integral part of our manner of life, we may fall before our own Egypts and Gerars and discover how little faith we actually have.

In Abraham's case I believe God in sovereign providence allowed these events to happen to him so he would recognize his need of complete dependence on God rather than upon his own ingenuity. Like Abraham, we need to learn that our faith must be in God, not in our faith—and certainly not in our cleverness.

Another major test of Abraham's faith came in connection with the birth of Isaac. To fulfill His covenant promise, God would have to perform a miracle. Sarah was barren, and Abraham was so old he probably could no longer father a child (Hebrews 11:11). God promised Abraham and Sarah a son, but they both knew very well that, naturally speaking, this event was impossible. In fact, Sarah was overcome with laughter. Despite her subsequent denial, she thought it ridiculous that the strangers who made the announcement to Abraham and her apparently did not know that after a certain age women cannot bear children (Genesis 18:12-15).

In confronting this latest test of their faith, Abraham and Sarah had already attempted to help God out by finding some natural or normal way for His covenant promise to be fulfilled. They agreed to have Hagar become Abraham's second wife (Genesis 16:1, 2). Out of that relationship was born Ishmael, the apparent solution to what seemed an impossible situation.

Many have been the lamentable and tragic consequences of this contrived solution. The implacable hostility that prevails today between Jew and Arab is but the current manifestation of an antipathy as ancient as that between their progenitors Isaac and Ishmael, Sarah and Hagar (see Genesis 21:8-10).

The lesson is clear. If God has made a promise we think is impossible, we should place our faith in God and not try to figure out ways in which we think we may help Him out of His supposed dilemma.

At Drew University some years ago I was reviewing a program being offered there. One of the staff came to me and said he understood I was from Wheaton College. Then he remarked that he had been involved in an evangelistic campaign allegedly conducted by one of our graduates. He said that when it came time for the invitation, the evangelist wanted to make sure people would come forward. To encourage this, the speaker had hired a number of college students who were instructed to get up out of their seats and walk down to the front as soon as the invitation was given. They were supposed to "prime the pump," so others would come. To this day I have been reluctant to believe this incident, but the staff member insisted the story was true. I still hope it was not.

One of our sons gave a somewhat similar report about the way an evangelistic group handled the close of a meeting he had attended. The leader asked everyone to bow in prayer and then invited those present to receive Christ and to indicate this by raising their hands. Then the evangelist said, "Thank you, I see your hand, I see your hand." Out of curiosity our son did not shut his eyes, and he saw no hands raised at that time. Yet the evangelist kept saying, "I see your hand," and eventually a few hands did go up.

What could be the possible rationalization for such procedures?

Any person who thus manipulates others is indicating that the Spirit of God cannot adequately move people without the aid of some kind of contrivance. That seemed to be Abraham's and Sarah's point of view.

An Amazing Illustration of Faith

After the birth of Isaac, Abraham faced another test of faith that has a poignancy with which every father can identify. I have imagined taking our son, Taylor, by the hand and saying, "Taylor, we are going for a walk up the mountain." He would note, "You have a knife and some wood and matches. Why are we taking these up the mountain?" "Son, we are going to offer a sacrifice." "But, Daddy, we have the wood and the matches and the knife, but we don't have any lamb for the sacrifice."

At that point I suspect I would get so choked up that I could say no more. That is why I admire Abraham's being able to continue, saying, "God himself will provide the lamb for the burnt offering, my son" (Genesis 22:8). To me, this is an amazing illustration of faith. Abraham obeyed without question when he got the perplexing command from God to take his only son, the one who was to be the fulfillment of God's promises, and offer him on the mountain.

Why was Abraham able to have such confidence? I think he reasoned that a God who could take the bodies of Sarah and himself and make them productive again was capable of performing another miracle in the dead body of Isaac (see Hebrews 11:19). So he was willing to obey God.

Furthermore, Abraham really did not have an alternate covenant child in Ishmael. The *New Internation Version* renders Hebrews 11:17 this way: "He who had received the promises was about to sacrifice his one and only son." In this situation Ishmael did not count. Isaac was the only one, Abraham's sole option.

We should thank God that the faith of Abraham, as Romans 4 tells us, can be our faith as well. Both Romans 4 and Galatians 3 point out that the kind of faith Abraham exercised is the kind you and I are given to enable us to enter into spiritual life. And then, when by faith we become children of Abraham (Galatians 3:7), we should manifest the same quality of faith he had in trusting God for Isaac's restoration to life. A spiritually dead person can be made spiritually alive, and a spiritually vital person can live in obedience to God, trusting consistently in His faithfulness.

In all our relationships with others, we should be known as people who trust God and obey His Word. Any losses or setbacks we may experience because of our faith are, in my judgment, worth it all if we are rightly related to God. As we maintain our spiritual integrity, He will work out His purposes for His glory and for our benefit.

9

Shaping a Leader

The late Secretary of State John Foster Dulles traveled so extensively that someone suggested President Eisenhower tell him, "Don't just do something; stand there!" But more often the would-be leader is immobilized by indecision; he neither knows what to do nor how to do it.

By contrast Moses, one of the greatest leaders in Biblical history, superbly demonstrated the delicate balance between awareness of the need to act and submission to the will of God. This interaction resulted from the blend of his natural gifts, spiritual enduement, and experience in walking with God.

Stephen made reference to elements of this in his great and final sermon:

> At that time Moses was born, and he was no ordinary child ["and was exceeding fair," KJV]. For three months he was cared for in his father's house. When he was placed outside, Pharaoh's daughter took him and brought him up as her own son. Moses was educated in all the wisdom of the Egyptians and was powerful in speech and action. (Acts 7:20-22)

Natural Endowments

Although specific attributes differ, a leader has natural endowments. Moses was a beautiful child who was specially favored in the sight of the Lord. In addition to being physically attractive, Moses had a higher than average intellect. Scripture says he was skilled in all the considerable wisdom of the Egyptians. But he was no abstract theorist, as Stephen pointed out:

> When Moses was forty years old, he decided to visit his fellow Israelites. He saw one of them being mistreated by an Egyptian, so he went to his defense and avenged him by killing the Egyptian. (Acts 7:23, 24)

A Sense of Timing

Because one of Moses' endowments was concern and compassion, his emotions were aroused when he saw one of the Israelites being beaten. Moses was moved by injustice, a reaction requisite to true leadership. Sensing the dynamic of the moment, he acted decisively. Moses determined that the only way to defend his countryman was to attack the Egyptian. While this is an extreme example, it illustrates the fact that the moment for action must be perceived and utilized or the opportunity will be lost.

The history of the evangelical movement in the United States during the second half of the twentieth century provides a number of examples of how the dynamic of the moment was perceived and utilized. During this period such organizations as Inter-Varsity Christian Fellowship, Campus Crusade, Youth for Christ, Young Life, and Navigators were formed to reach students and other special groups. The most massive translation effort in modern history was launched by Cameron Townsend and Wycliffe Bible Translators. The Officers Christian Fellowship, together with Navigators and a division of Campus Crusade, targeted the Armed Forces. The enormous potential of radio and later television was perceived by the World Radio Missionary Fellowship (HCJB), the Far Eastern Broadcasting Company, and Trans World Radio, to say nothing of the rise of the so-called televangelists.

Evangelism's most effective representative was and is Dr. Billy Graham, who seized the initiative to form a multi-faceted ministry and selected a capable staff to run it. He and Dr. Harold Ockenga recognized the need for an evangelical magazine and began *Christianity Today*. Then they became part of the implementation of Fuller Seminary in the west and Gordon-Conwell Seminary in the east. Dr. Ockenga was also one of the visionaries who conceived and helped organize the National Association of Evangelicals in 1942. Essential to all of this progress was the recognition of a need, the sanctified imagination to devise ways to meet it, and the availability of resources and technology that translated the conceptual into the possible and actual.

But there is another factor that may not be so obvious and about which there may not be concurrence. Let me state this thesis: *God, for His own inscrutable purposes, ordains certain periods as times of special blessing and outreach.*

Kenneth Scott Latourette, in his multi-volume work on the expansion of Christianity, called the 1800s "The Great Century." The Wesleyan Revival that swept England during the last part of the eighteenth century seems today to have been strategic in sparing that country from the excesses of the French Revolution. Similarly, the Protestant Reformation was a time of extraordinary ecclesiastical and theological activity the benefits of which we still enjoy today. Yet in those times who would have thought that a discredited preacher or an obscure monk would, under God, make such amazing impact!

Does God's foreknowledge lessen our responsibility to exploit a strategic opportunity? Not at all. But our sovereign God, as William Cowper put it, moves in mysterious ways His wonders to perform. Thus I suggest that vision, purpose, and blessing remain as necessary elements in responding to the dynamics of the moment, but always under the sovereign hand of God.

Spiritual Enduements

Although blessed with natural endowments that prompted decisive action, Moses was also given spiritual enduements by God. These capabilities surfaced early, developed systematically, and were especially manifested to God's people in Moses' later years. His spiritual perspective—i.e., his being attuned to God's timing—and his sense of priorities are among the attributes that helped to accredit Moses' leadership. His natural endowments came to blend beautifully with his spiritual enduements.

My wife and I have been blessed with five children. What has impressed us, among other things, is how different they are one from another. Having the same parents and the same environment up to their teen years, they nevertheless have distinctive and contrasting traits of personality and temperament. Yet all are endowed with above-average intelligence, musical capabilities (inherited and acquired from their mother), articulateness, and pleasing personalities. So they do have both similar and distinct natural endowments.

Each of our children has had a determination to develop his or her natural endowments. It is here that it may be a bit difficult to distinguish between those gifts and abilities that are natural and just need development and those special skills that are the supernatural provision of the Holy Spirit.

Bezalel and Oholiab were given particular capabilities by God through the filling of His Holy Spirit (Exodus 31:1-6 and 36:1). This suggests that such bestowment may be in the area of craftsmanship as well as in more emotional or psychological characteristics such as love, patience, gentleness, or self-control. In addition, the listing of the gifts of the Holy Spirit in Romans 12:6-8 and 1 Corinthians 12:7-11 includes a number that are directly related to leadership, such as serving, teaching, encouraging, governing, showing mercy, having wisdom, knowledge, and faith.

Blending the Natural and Supernatural

A Christian leader's realistic self-appraisal will disclose a blending of the natural and the supernatural consistent with the particular calling God has given him. Such recognition should, on the one hand, prompt a sense of gratitude for the Lord's enablement and, on the other hand, elicit the less common but still essential awareness that such capabilities must be exercised with scrupulous stewardship and sensitivity. Confidence in decision-making—though a refreshing contrast to maddening diffidence—can also manifest itself in impulsiveness or arbitrariness. Diligence in governing can overlook compassion or concern that probes behind a mistake or poor performance to ascertain the root of the problem. A dynamic personality can become a tool to exploit and manipulate others or to structure programs and procedures to produce the maximum favorable exposure.

I believe keeping a proper balance depends on a right focus. If the focus is on the needs and problems of others, the endowments and gifts will be employed in loving service. If it is upon the status and reputation of the leader, the resources will be denied others and lavished upon self, with any modification calculated to accrue to the leader's benefit. For the Christian leader the task is precise: to serve others for God's glory and their benefit.

A Vision of Outcome

Scripture reports that Moses, "when he had grown up" (Hebrews 11:24), exhibited maturity in both natural capabilities and spiritual enduement.

> He chose to be mistreated along with the people of God rather than to enjoy the pleasures of sin for a short time. He regarded disgrace for the sake of Christ as of greater value than the treasures of Egypt, because he was looking ahead to his reward . . . he persevered because he saw him who is invisible. (vv. 25-27)

An admiral who was a Christian once suggested that in going to a new assignment, the first thing one ought do is to run up his flag; i.e., we should announce our identity with Jesus Christ. In his crisis of allegiance, Moses ran up his flag. He chose to reject the option of going along with the prevailing culture; he spurned the current climate of opinion. Instead, he identified himself with the despised minority who followed the Lord.

Scripture says Moses acted in this decisive way because he considered his future reward. In other words, Moses had a spiritual perspective—a clear-eyed vision of the One whom he served and of the eternal recompense that only He can give.

Because he had killed the Egyptian, Moses at this point had to flee Egypt and for forty years live on the back side of the desert. Superficially we might pronounce these as wasted years. But on the contrary, they were years of preparation for Moses and were also the exact interval of time that was necessary until the conditions were right for the deliverance of God's people. This experience of Moses suggests a generalization that has significant Scriptural support: *God will select us for a task only when we are ready and the conditions are right for the position He has for us.*

When Moses attempted to act on his own, neither was he ready, nor were the conditions right. But when God called Moses out of the wilderness, the sovereign purposes of the Lord were fulfilled in accordance with the divine timetable. God waited forty years until Moses' pride and desire for status and all the other things characteristic of Egypt were put in their proper place. During that time Moses learned patience and humility and the ability to step aside and have no status whatsoever. I do not believe Moses expected ever again to return to the recognition he previously enjoyed.

It is one thing to become successful. It is quite another to go down after having been up. Can the leader endure God's test to determine the quality of his dedication? Is he capable on the basis of principle to go into isolation and obscurity for the cause to which he has given himself?

Remember that even our Lord Jesus Christ was about thirty years of age when He began His public ministry. Some might state that had He started any sooner, He would not have been accepted in that culture. Perhaps this is so. Yet I believe that in some mysterious way even our Savior in His humanity had to wait thirty years, after condescending to become a man, before He was ready to begin His public ministry.

A second generalization about God's call of an individual may be more difficult to accept. But as I read Scripture, it seems to me that in many instances the following is true: *Even if we initiate inquiries or applications, it is God who summons the leader to the position rather than the leader who generates the opportunity.*

Moses was not looking for a place of leadership. In fact, he needed considerable persuading to go back to Egypt. He went only because God opened the way and promised to be with him. The Lord knew that the circumstances were just right and that He could use Moses for His glory.

The experience of Joseph (Genesis 37, 39—50) provides another illustration of this idea. After his God-given dreams predicted a leadership role, he faced one setback after another. If anything, the circumstances seemed to contradict his dreams. Yet at just the right time in history God opened the way for Joseph to assume the promised leadership role. Clearly, only the Lord could have ordered circumstances in such a way.

In my own career, the striking thing has been that I have yet to seek a position. When I left the Navy to go to graduate school to prepare for the mission field, I was offered a part-time teaching position at Wheaton, which I accepted. Later I was approached to go to Gordon College. While there I received an invitation to minister in a church in New Hampshire.

The New Hampshire invitation came about in an interesting way.

I had gone to the campus to pick up my mail when the librarian "happened," as we would say, to step out into the hall and see me. He said that his cousin had just called from Manchester, New Hampshire, to say that their pastor had suffered a heart attack. He asked if I would be willing to minister for three or four Sundays. I agreed.

Each Lord's Day the family and I drove to Manchester. After four weeks we said good-bye to the people, as the pastor seemed sufficiently recovered to resume his duties. But within a month they called us again, told us that the pastor had suffered a second heart attack, and asked if we would come back. We did. In early May the pastor died.

We were scheduled to sail for China that summer, but we had no housing until the time we were to leave. So we moved into the parsonage. When conditions in China prevented our sailing, the church wanted us to remain even while we commuted from Manchester to Harvard to study Chinese.

When our mission asked us to resign because their missionaries were being withdrawn from China, the president of Gordon College offered me another position on the faculty. We moved to Brockton, Massachusetts, and began attending an evangelical church there. In the spring of 1951, the pastor told me he had resigned and wondered if I would preach for a few Sundays until the church could call another minister. I told him I would be glad to fill in. So I preached for four months while the church contacted several ministers, all of whom turned them down.

Finally in September the church asked if I would continue if they hired a full-time assistant. I agreed and continued for three and a half years, preaching in the church on Sundays and working at the college on weekdays. Despite the stress of those years, I learned many valuable lessons.

During that time Gordon's president asked me to serve as acting dean of the college for three months. I agreed to try. In May he requested that I continue as dean, which I did for ten years.

When the president of Gordon died and a new president was appointed, we were visited by Dr. Edman from Wheaton College. Just as he was leaving campus I happened to remark that I thought the Lord was "lifting the cloud" at Gordon, although I was not sure where He wanted me to go. He responded by asking me to come to Wheaton to teach. After much prayer I accepted. When I had taught at Wheaton for a year and a half, Dr. Edman appointed me his administrative assistant in academics, and less than two years later I was advised that the board of trustees was considering me for the presidency of Wheaton College, an office I assumed in 1965.

I have had similar experiences with the presidency of the National Association of Evangelicals and of the World Evangelical Fellowship and with my position as Vice President of the Quarryville Presbyterian Retirement Home in Pennsylvania. I mention these things simply to say that in our experience God graciously has provided opportunities we did not seek, but which He made available to us. That is why I am convinced we can always trust the providence of God for assignments that are right for us.

Consider now a third generalization: *When God calls an individual and gives him a job to do, He will supernaturally provide the capabilities needed for that specific job.*

When God called Moses in the back side of the desert, Moses was dramatically different from the person he had been in Egypt. Once he had been mighty in words and in deeds. But when the Lord called him forty years later, Moses pointed out that he was "slow of speech" (Exodus 4:10). This might be explained as the result of his not having talked much for forty years and of his not having shouldered any demanding leadership responsibilities during those decades. For whatever reason, Moses needed special enablement for the work God was calling him to do.

To accommodate Moses' fears, the Lord designated Aaron to be his mouthpiece—at first. Early in the Exodus account it speaks of "Aaron and Moses," but soon the wording is reversed to "Moses and

Aaron." Moses increasingly did the speaking. In fact, he acquired not simply an ability to be articulate but the capacity to utter an authoritative word of leadership.

In summary, then, a leader has both natural and supernatural gifts. He is prepared by God for just the right moment to assume his leadership role. When that time comes, God will open the door of opportunity. God will also provide whatever special enduements are necessary to that calling.

The leader's responsibility is to be available, teachable, and responsible in fulfilling the assignment God gives.

10

The Shaping Continues ...

A
s the Christian leader becomes progressively more teachable and shoulders additional responsibility, he inevitably must learn how to delegate tasks and supervise personnel. Exodus 18 provides a case study in management technique. Jethro, once he was on the scene to visit his son-in-law Moses, saw from his detached perspective how overworked Moses was.

> ... Moses took his seat to serve as judge for the people, and they stood around him from morning till evening. ... He [Jethro] said, "What is this you are doing for the people? Why do you alone sit as judge, while all these people stand around you from morning till evening? ... The work is too heavy for you; you cannot handle it alone." (vv. 13-18)

One of the perils in administrative leadership is the tendency to become caught up in the minutiae of the job and thus be unable to maintain sufficient perspective to deal with the major concerns of the enterprise. For this reason, Jethro urged Moses to appoint qualified men to be his subordinates.

Criteria for Selection
Exodus 18:21 furnishes the basic qualifications for appointment. Moses was to employ associates who (1) feared God, (2) were men

of truth, and (3) hated covetousness or dishonest gain. These are excellent criteria by which to select qualified subordinates today too.

Those who must employ non-Christians may object that such individuals do not fear God. Yet even some non-Christians have high moral and ethical standards, respect God, and have a willingness to acknowledge His sovereignty. And of course Christians should especially have profound reverence for the sovereign God.

It is an obvious advantage to have associates who will speak and live the truth, but an administrative blight to be told what others think you want to hear rather than what is so. Men of truth not only state the facts to their associates in dealing with an issue, but they also speak the truth to their superiors. Yet the one who speaks the truth must have a criterion to which to relate the specific issues.

The theologian Dooyeweerd, in the Netherlands, is reported to have recommended that Christians read the Scriptures so regularly and with such understanding as to soak themselves in truth. When any particular issue confronts a Scripture-soaked individual, he will be able immediately to think Biblically and to apply pertinent Scriptural principles to the specific problem.

The third criterion for subordinates is that they hate covetousness (NIV "dishonest gain," the outcome of covetousness). We usually think of covetousness as a problem resulting from a love of money. But it includes more. Some leaders have had subordinates who so coveted a higher position that they were prepared to discredit their superiors, just as Absalom did David. I distinguish this stance from a natural ambition to better oneself and to be prepared for the next higher position. Rather, covetousness in this context is an inordinate ambition that constantly depreciates the leader so the subordinate can appear more and more as *the* man for the situation. An identifying phrase often is "if only . . ." "If only I were president . . . if only I were the pastor . . . if only I were the manager, I would handle things the way they should be handled."

As in the case of Absalom, such covetousness results in an

endeavor to capture the loyalties and affections of the people. The leader, therefore, should choose subordinates who will not be covetous in this way but will serve effectively in their particular echelon. Qualified subordinates are essential for the success of any enterprise.

Fortunate indeed is the leader whose colleagues love truth and hate covetousness.

Serving One Another

Before an associate can work effectively and efficiently, he needs to know how his leader regards him. One of the procedures recommended by some students of management is to have the leader say to the subordinate, "How may I be of help to you?" At first this query seems to contradict the notion that subordinates are the helpers of the leader, a view widely held by both executives and staff. Yet the recommendation fits in well with the characterization of leaders in Scripture. The idea of serving is part of the expectation for those who are called to be the shepherds of God's flock (1 Peter 5:2) as they model the ministry of the Chief Shepherd (v. 4).

This concept is also found in Romans 13. In this passage rulers are represented as serving God by serving those under their care (v. 6). Recognize also that the good advice given King Rehoboam—which he rejected, to his own detriment—was that he, as a perceptive monarch, should "be a servant to these people and serve them . . ." (1 Kings 12:7). Then he would find that the people would in turn serve him.

But how can we serve our subordinates or be a help to them? First of all, we need to know them well, and this happens only after thoughtful observation and careful analysis. No matter how similar a team of associates may appear, they have differences that must be taken into account in dealing with them. An utterly candid, direct approach may be just what one person requires, while another will be threatened and inhibited by it. By the same token, what may appear to some as a deliberate and measured procedure may drive an activist colleague "up the wall."

I have practiced and recommended sustained individual interaction with each key associate, believing there is no other way to gain the requisite insights. The subordinate also needs to know without equivocation that he has the leader's support, even when a mistake is made.

At the same time, not entirely in jest I told my key administrators they were allowed one mistake but not two or more of the same kind. The point is, we should pursue increasing efficiency. The leader needs to ensure, however, that whatever is required to enable his colleagues to avoid making the same mistake twice is provided. Sometimes this includes clearer instructions, better staff work, or more careful delegation. I have learned that intensive knowledge of the strengths and limitations of my key associates was essential to the proper exercise of my role as leader/helper.

Once a good working relationship is established, the leader should provide "shade," as one successful executive put it. What he meant was that the leader positively would promote the best interests of his subordinates and also defend his colleagues against unwarranted opposition. Fortunate indeed is the individual who rests in the security of his leader's strength and influence.

One particular application of this is the giving of a deserved word of praise for a task well done. Commendation is clearly Scriptural, as seen in our Lord's Parable of the Talents and His Parable of the Ten Minas (Matthew 25:14-30 and Luke 19:11-27). Few things can negatively impact morale more than the absence of recognition of work well done or the conveying of the impression that the best one can do is never good enough. I do not advocate so-called "stroking," but I do urge justified praise.

Delegating Responsibility

Assigning responsibilities to subordinates does not relieve the leader of his responsibility to set basic policy. Jethro specified to Moses that he must

"Teach them the decrees and laws, and show them the way to live and the duties they are to perform." (Exodus 18:20)

The leader is responsible both to enunciate general policy and to provide management training.

For years I was content to set basic policy, assuming that the management team knew their jobs. Then, when I took some management training myself, I came to realize the necessity of making sure the administrative group understood procedures as well as policies. On this basis they could establish their priorities and achieve the general objectives.

I have found this procedure helpful. Each year I would construct a series of goals for myself. At the end of the year I would share with my key subordinates my appraisal of my own performance and ask for their perspective on this performance. Then I gave them what I perceived to be realistic goals for the coming year and asked them in turn to share these with *their* subordinates. In this way the goals I eventually set would be the collective responsibility of the management team, not just of the president. Thus when I worked on my goals I had the support of the vice presidents and their subordinates.

Moses led in a similar manner. He established the objectives and goals for the group, shared them with his associates, and instructed them so they would know how to carry out the general policies he had set. Keep in mind that this does not relieve the leader of ultimate accountability. It simply means that by delegation he can do his work better.

The time saved by delegation must be guarded or it can easily be dissipated. I did not take any phone calls from 8—9 A.M. I reserved that period to plan the day and to think about the best way to use my time and energies. It is helpful to ask yourself each day, Which matters can only I handle? Colleagues should be given the freedom to do whatever they can do, *even if in some cases you could do the task better yourself.*

I had to tell myself that I was not going to be in my position indefinitely and that others should learn to take responsibility. They even learned about the functions that were mine alone, so that if an emergency called me away they could handle them effectively.

Delegation (again see Matthew 25:14-30 and Luke 19:11-27) seems to be a principle in the kingly rule of our Lord, for He has assigned to us such important tasks as evangelism, nurturing, caring for His creation, and generally carrying out His commands. I find it remarkable that the Lord trusts us with such a considerable amount of responsibility and never abandons us or sets us adrift. The fact that we are even permitted on occasion to make mistakes suggests that our Master wants us to grow and mature, something every Christian manager should want for his administrative team.

What is important in the matter of delegation is a periodic review—*accountability*. Even the best of us needs this. A friend of mine says that most people do not do what they are expected to do; they do what they are *inspected* to do. Like any generalization, this one has its notable exceptions. But it is interesting how easily most of us slacken off when nobody is noticing and how quickly we recover when we know someone is going to review our work. Certain exceptional people work well independently without being reviewed, but many people make an extra effort when they know somebody is coming by to see them.

Holding a subordinate accountable not only helps the leader but the subordinate as well. Measurable expectations provide a degree of security and focus greatly to be preferred to the bewildering uncertainty of not knowing what is expected. Here we can learn much from God's dealings with His people. Clear directives and specific expectations are to be found in both the Old and New Testaments. And the certainty that our performance will be evaluated by the Lord has a salutary effect on our stewardship of time and opportunity. The same constructive certainty is essential to Christian enterprises as well.

Utilizing Spiritual Perspective

Not only did Moses establish his leadership by taking responsibility for basic policy and by learning how to delegate effectively, but he also firmly held to a spiritual perspective. Exodus 32 gives us the description of a series of circumstances which disclose the depth and scope of his devotion not only to the Lord but also to the children of Israel. To be sure, the circumstances are not unique. They have occurred in the lives of many others who have been called to Christian leadership. But Moses' example here is an inspiring one for us all.

While he was still on the mountain with the Lord, Moses learned what was going on back in the camp, and thus he was not surprised when he returned. He knew very well that the people were disobedient. They had rejected both him and the things for which he stood. More significantly, he knew Israel was acting contrary to the Law God had just given to him; they were rejecting Him.

The remarkable thing to me is that before Moses left the mountain and after he had been made aware of the fact that the people had rejected him, God put him to the test, especially when He said, "Now leave me alone so that my anger may burn against them and I may destroy them. Then I will make you into a great nation" (v. 10).

Notice the test here. Moses had just been told that the people he had been leading in the wilderness had repudiated the things for which he stood. Then God offered to destroy them and make Moses' descendants into a great nation (vv. 9, 10). In response (vv. 11-13) Moses manifested his impressive capability to utilize a spiritual perspective. He was able to see things in clear focus. His outlook was not so provincial or circumscribed that he saw everything in the light of his own interest.

We can rejoice in how triumphantly Moses passed the test, not allowing personal ambition to distort his perspective. Specifically his response was one of compassionate supplication.

But Moses sought the favor of the Lord his God. "O Lord," he said, "why should your anger burn against your people, whom you brought out of Egypt with great power and a mighty hand? Why should the Egyptians say, 'It was with evil intent that he brought them out, to kill them in the mountains and to wipe them off the face of the earth'? Turn from your fierce anger; relent and do not bring disaster on your people. Remember your servants Abraham, Isaac and Israel, to whom you swore by your own self: 'I will make your descendants as numerous as the stars in the sky and I will give your descendants all this land I promised them, and it will be their inheritance forever.'"

Observe how completely detached from personal ambition Moses was. Even when he was offered a most remarkable possibility, he viewed it in light of the Lord's great covenant promises to His people and of their reputation as the Lord's servants. Thus he, so to speak, said to God, "Thank You very much, but I would plead with You not to do what You have suggested." This is the mark of a spiritually minded leader whose own ambition does not distort his perception of God's purposes for the enterprise in which he is involved.

Is Any Ambition Proper?

Is all ambition, then, unwarranted? Must it of necessity foreshorten perspective or limit vision? When an opportunity presents itself, conventional wisdom says the leader should seize the initiative and achieve the objective. But is this all there is to it? *For the Christian, there is more.* In particular, there are guidelines to be drawn from Scripture to provide the leader with an appropriate perspective.

First of all, there are the assurances that God opens the door for us at the right time and that He has promised to guide and equip us for the new challenge. Solomon illustrates this in his reaction to the circumstances surrounding his accession to the kingship and his being gifted by God for the exercise of his leadership (1 Kings 1—3).

His experience also highlights the need for decisive action consistent with divine calling.

Scripture also teaches that to desire a leadership position is to set one's heart on a good work (1 Timothy 3:1—"If anyone sets his heart on being an overseer, he desires a noble task"). Yet at least two emphases must also be drawn from this same passage that are normative in the justifiable exercise of ambition. First, there should have been a demonstration of responsible action in the tasks previously undertaken by the prospective leader. Second, the orientation of the individual must be toward ministry and service to the glory of God for the benefit of those who are under the leader's care and direction.

I submit that when a leader keeps in mind the sovereign direction of God and His provision of both opportunity and ability, *then* ambition can be pursued. Further, when opposition arises or frustrations develop, the leader with this perspective can exercise patience and as necessary reorient his priorities since he is confident God is in control. But when ambition becomes intensely personal, dictatorship replaces leadership, and alienation supplants inspiration and trust.

The tragic account of King Saul in 1 Samuel 13—15 is a major illustration of these things, as are the events leading up to his death. By contrast, the priest Phinehas was commended by God "because he was zealous for the honor of his God" (Numbers 25:13). A similar attitude may be seen in the lives of John the Baptist (John 3:30— "He [Jesus] must become greater; I must become less") and the Apostle Paul (Colossians 1:18—". . . that in everything he [Christ] might have the supremacy").

I am persuaded that when our ambition misdirects glory and praise to us rather than to the Lord, He may very well permit barrenness, failure, or even death to come our way, for He will not share His glory with another (see Isaiah 48:11 and the account of Herod in Acts 12:21-23).

It is difficult to trace a precise cause-and-effect relationship in some of the highly publicized failures of prominent Christian leaders.

There is at least a reasonable assumption, however, that God may have left them to themselves in order to teach them how vulnerable they could become when they were too self-confident and self-centered.

Or the barrenness and powerlessness may have resulted from the wrong kind of nurturing—the bolstering of men's egos when all eyes are upon them and they sense people are hanging on their every word. Too often the craving for this kind of emotional reinforcement prompts a leader to "work" a group, telling them what he knows they enjoy hearing, or entertaining rather than edifying them.

I do not have in mind here the elimination of all humorous elements from our presentations, but I do question the primary emphasis being on the cleverly crafted phrase or story rather than on that which has a direct relationship to Biblical truth. Further, I believe a leader should avoid misusing Scripture and thus causing people to laugh at God's Word.

Our ambition should be to serve and minister in such a way that our greatest fulfillment comes from the witness of the Holy Spirit to and then through us and from the anticipation of the "Well done" of our sovereign Lord. Hence, Christian ambition is a combination of vision, opportunity, stewardship, and self-effacement. Whatever we do should be done for the glory of God (1 Corinthians 10:31).

As I have said, the selective use of well-chosen management seminars was something I found to be helpful to my staff. Such sessions provided a common ground of understanding regarding procedures and practices.

I also wanted to help my key associates grasp the Biblical and theological principles that are essential to a Christian enterprise. To accomplish this, I asked them to read the systematic theology written by a former Wheaton College president, Dr. J. Oliver Buswell, Jr., and to do additional reading in the area of the integration of faith and learning.

To me it is essential that Christians seek to act Biblically in the vocations to which God has called them. The perceptive Christian leader will recognize this need personally and will want to inspire his associates by both precept and example in the pursuit of this objective. That is what was evident in the life of Moses. May this be said of us as well.

11

... And the Shaping
Goes On

We have been considering the shaping of the leader Moses. Let us learn some further lessons from that man's life and experience with God, beginning with a subject that is often misunderstood or even openly mocked today.

A Look at Meekness

Only those who are meek can consistently maintain a spiritual perspective that is undistorted by overweening ambition. Numbers 12:3 declares that ". . . the man Moses was very meek, above all the men which were upon the face of the earth" (KJV). Such meekness stands in contrast to the popular conception of this quality. When I was a boy the newspapers carried a comic-strip character called Casper Milquetoast. Casper was weak, ineffective, painfully shy, and retiring. He was the kind of person who would knock at a door and hope no one would answer because he feared any kind of confrontation whatsoever. That is the popular caricature of meekness.

Nor is this distortion absent from common perceptions of Christ. The passage that says, "Take my yoke upon you and learn from me, for I am gentle [KJV "meek"] and humble in heart" (Matthew 11:29) is too often linked with "Gentle Jesus, meek and mild/You were once a little child." Thus some religionists portray the Lord Jesus with a thin, ascetic face and a passive demeanor, incapable of doing anything bold or decisive.

But that is not what the New Testament records. The One who claimed, "I am gentle and humble in heart" was the same One who strode into the Temple with a whip, overturned the money changers' tables, and declared that these people were not to make His Father's house a place of thievery.

Why is this One characterized as meek? It is because the Biblical definition of meekness is radically different from the popular conception. *Meekness in Scripture is an uncompromising subordination to the will of God so that His will is primary in the life of the individual.*

Thus the Lord Jesus could declare, "I seek not to please myself but him who sent me" (John 5:30).

Taking Decisive Action

Similarly Moses could affirm, in effect, that he wanted to do everything in order to please God. That explains the behavior of this meek man as he came down from the mountain.

> And he took the calf they had made and burned it in the fire; then he ground it to powder, scattered it on the water and made the Israelites drink it. (Exodus 32:20)

What a dramatic scene that must have been, with group after group bending down to drink, some protesting, but all obeying, as Moses stood there with stern face and burning eye.

Dealing with Aaron

Moses dealt next with his brother, Aaron, who had been left in charge. Interestingly enough, Aaron's response was to try to put the blame on the people.

"Do not be angry, my lord," Aaron answered. "You know how prone these people are to evil. They said to me, 'Make us gods who will go before us. As for this fellow Moses who brought us up out of Egypt, we don't know what has happened to him.' So I told them, 'Whoever has any gold jewelry, take it off.' Then they gave me the gold, and I threw it into the fire, and out came this calf!" (Exodus 32:22-24)

I can imagine Moses saying, "Aaron, are you telling me that this engraved calf just *happened* to come out of the fire?" As usual, a lame excuse was worse than none at all. Moses was fully justified in rebuking his brother. Aaron had permitted himself to be manipulated by circumstances and public opinion, behavior which is the very opposite of Biblical meekness.

Imagine yourself in this situation. What if your congregation or your people or those under your authority completely turned away from what you knew was right and your assistant joined in with them? Some would be tempted, in the interest of harmony, to overlook the whole thing. But this option is not open to the Biblically meek leader.

In dealing forthrightly with the people, Moses called out those in the group who apparently had not followed the majority and ordered them to impose judgment on the flagrantly disobedient. Three thousand people died because Moses, a meek person, understood that a vital principle was involved: the sovereignty of God had been challenged. For that reason the same man who pleaded with God on the mountain not to destroy the people made them drink the polluted water and then executed those who were the most flagrant in their behavior.

We must recognize the leadership principle involved here. A leader must not be out to win a popularity contest but to uphold the ideals he is obliged in integrity to maintain. If this involves the rebuke or the punishment of subordinates, then such action must be taken for the sake of the cause to which the leader is committed.

Do you know what too often happens at this point? Unless they have the extraordinary quality Moses had, some leaders who are involved in inflicting judgment on others find that their sensitivities become dulled and they get a perverse pleasure out of watching people squirm. Inflicting punishment can harden us to the point where we become less than our best.

A True Role Model

The very opposite was true of Moses. He was magnificent as he went to the Lord:

> "Oh, what a great sin these people have committed! They have made themselves gods of gold. But now, please forgive their sin—but if not, then blot me out of the book you have written." · (Exodus 32:31, 32)

Do you see the consistency here? On the mountain Moses would not accept the proposition that the people be destroyed so God could make of him a great nation. He also refused to countenance evil, knowing it too was inconsistent with the will and purpose of God. But he did not allow his feelings to cause him to reject Aaron and the people. Rather, he offered to be judged in their place if only God would spare them.

I am reminded of the Apostle Paul's statement that he could wish himself accursed for his kinsmen, his brethren according to the flesh (Romans 9:1-3). These for whom he yearned were the very people who hounded him from city to city and who tried repeatedly to have him killed. Yet he was able to say that he would forfeit his eternal destiny in their place if that were possible.

The mark of the Christian leader is a meekness that is gentle and yet also bold and decisive in standing for God's Word and God's reputation. It should also be a meekness sufficiently detached to feel no sense of vindictiveness or personal ambition. And it is a willingness to be set aside if only the Lord's cause can be advanced.

Reaccrediting Leadership

It would be natural to suppose that Israel, in a chastened mood, would have learned their lesson, so that in the future they would accept Moses without questioning his leadership. Unfortunately, as we read on in the Word of God, we see this was not the case. From this we learn that even though something has been done for a group which indicates concern for them, they will not necessarily accept their leader from then on. Indeed, the reaction may in time be quite the opposite.

Rather than being bothered by the tendency of others toward mistrust, the Christian leader should recognize that even Christian groups will expect him to reaccredit his leadership, just as Israel expected Moses to do. They were God's chosen people, a unique group. Yet they expected that this man, who had literally put his life on the line for them and had given them such devoted and courageous leadership, should regularly reestablish his right to be their leader.

In his epistles Paul repeatedly reminded the church leaders of his care and concern for them and for all of God's people. See, for example, 1 Corinthians 4:1-5, 8-21. Or note his discourse on the rights of an apostle as recorded in chapter 9 and his indomitable faith described in 2 Corinthians 1:8-11. In fact, many references in 2 Corinthians suggest that Paul made a special effort to establish or reinforce his creditability, particularly as seen in chapters 10–12. His testimony in Philippians 4 was probably given for the same purpose.

Some may well find these highly personal and sometimes emotional declarations to be out of character for them. Yet the principle of reaccrediting seems so evident that it may be accepted as an expectation without necessarily imitating the particular procedure of even so eminent a model as the Apostle Paul.

Further, one must note the important distinction between reaccreditation and defensiveness (a fierce effort to gain by pressure what could rather be secured by persuasion). Peter tells us that our Lord did not react in angry defiance and recrimination (see 1 Peter 2:23) despite far more provocation to do so than we have. The Christian leader who accuses and threatens as a reaccrediting device has missed the point and is only documenting his immaturity and insecurity.

Aboard ship I had two captains who illustrated both sides of this matter. The first paced back and forth on the bridge shouting commands in rapid succession when we were executing maneuvers that should have been routine for one of his rank. His successor never raised his voice but repeatedly demonstrated that he was competent to handle virtually any situation. Frankly, we needed the reaccreditation of the commanding officer's role, and the latter splendidly provided it—not once, but regularly.

Reaccreditation is warranted not only because of the perverseness of a group such as the children of Israel but because disillusioned, frustrated or cynical individuals need the reassurance our action will provide for them. Even our loving Heavenly Father regularly blesses us in ways tangible enough that we are reassured He is still aware of our need and splendidly able to meet it. Since God really "owes" us nothing, it is a mark of His loving-kindness that He responds to our need for reassurance.

A High Standard of Accountability

The fact that God holds the leader to a high standard of accountability is directly related to reaccreditation of leadership. Not even Moses was exempt. The kind of reproach Moses encountered (see Numbers 20) was surprising, especially in light of the blessings and miracles Israel had already experienced under his administration. The people's outburst was calculated to lacerate his feelings.

Now there was no water for the community, and the people gathered in opposition to Moses and Aaron. They quarreled with Moses and said, "If only we had died when our brothers fell dead before the Lord! Why did you bring the Lord's community into this desert, that we and our livestock should die here? Why did you bring us up out of Egypt to this terrible place? It has no grain or figs, grapevines or pomegranates. And there is no water to drink!" (vv. 2-5).

In reaction to these words, Moses permitted his exasperation to get the better of him, and he struck the rock rather than speaking to it as God had commanded. While God was gracious to provide the needed water anyway, He also held His servant accountable for his disobedience, as explained in verse 12:

But the Lord said to Moses and Aaron, "Because you did not trust in me enough to honor me as holy in the sight of the Israelites, you will not bring this community into the land I give them."

When Moses described this experience later, he disclosed that he asked the Lord if he could at least cross the Jordan to see the Promised Land.

At that time I pleaded with the Lord: "O sovereign Lord, you have begun to show to your servant your greatness and your strong hand. For what god is there in heaven or on earth who can do the deeds and mighty works you do? Let me go over and see the good land beyond the Jordan—that fine hill country and Lebanon." But because of you the Lord was angry with me and would not listen to me. "That is enough," the Lord said. "Do not speak to me anymore about this matter." (Deuteronomy 3:23-26)

One might ask whether a great leader who had guided the people through the wilderness to the edge of the Promised Land might not be excused for his momentary lapse of self-control. Or one might emphasize that Moses had done many good things and had been so consistent throughout almost all of his life that this one incident could be overlooked. As I have thought along these lines I have been reminded of this Scripture: "From everyone who has been given much, much will be demanded . . ." (Luke 12:48). Moses knew that in spite of the provocation of the people, he had been told to go out and *speak* to the rock. He knew also that in losing his temper he had stepped out of his position as a meek person. Instead of an uncompromising acceptance of the will and purpose of God, he chose to elevate himself and vent his displeasure on the people.

Moses' failure in this instance should be a warning to all of us in positions of Christian leadership. The more we grow in the Lord, enjoy the privileges He gives us, and rejoice in our opportunities to know His will and purpose, the more accountable we are to do what we know is right. Let us not offer the excuse that we were unfairly provoked; instead, let us pursue the cultivation of Biblical meekness and so maintain our self-control.

Furthermore, if we complain that the pressures are more than we can bear, and in so doing imply that the Lord cannot or will not help us, He may take us at our word and relieve us of our responsibilities. That was Elijah's experience, described in 1 Kings 19. After being threatened by Jezebel, Elijah fled into the wilderness and cried out, "I have had enough, Lord. Take my life; I am no better than my ancestors" (v. 4). In response, the Lord nourished him and then confronted him with the wind, the earthquake, the fire, and finally the still, small voice. In reply to the Lord's question, "What are you doing here, Elijah?" (v. 13), Elijah voiced his frustration that in spite of his faithfulness to the Lord he was in mortal danger and was the only one of the Lord's servants left. The reply Elijah received was striking. Among other things, God directed him to anoint Elisha to take his place in the prophetic ministry.

I suggest there may be a lesson to be learned from this incident. If we let our emotions get out of control, or if we complain to the Lord that we cannot take the pressure any longer, He is likely to take us at our word and instruct us to hand over our assignment to another. So sometimes (thankfully not all times) I have told the Lord, "O God, I do not know whether I can stand it any longer or not, but I am not saying I want to be relieved of my responsibilities. I know You are able and willing to help me, and I again submit to Your sovereignty over my life." To me, this is authentic meekness.

Meekness Clarified

As we keep in mind that our Lord is the supreme example of Biblical meekness, we can deduce that our behavior patterns which clearly conflict with His are indications we are not being meek. His complete submission to the Father's will is an accurate general description, but, fallible beings that we are, we need some particulars. Let me suggest a few.

Meekness, properly understood, enables a leader to *work within a prescribed set of principles and practices*, even as our Lord always did that which pleased the Father (John 5:30). He fulfilled the Father's will as He provided leadership for His disciples. Similarly, the Christian leader will both be subordinate to a God-ordained authority structure and lead effectively, in contrast to adopting the adversarial stance so common in today's world. I do not have in mind a passive acquiescence to that which is wrong or defective, but I am suggesting that constructive change can be effected without adopting a posture of defiance or imperiousness. This same principle applies to governing boards as well as to operating executives.

As stated before, another specific of Biblical meekness is *the absence of self-centeredness*. It may be superficial to describe our Lord simply as The Man For Others, but not untrue. A better and more

Biblical characterization is that He came to serve rather than be served and to give His life as a ransom for many (Matthew 20:28).

Such will be the orientation of the Christian leader who demonstrates Biblical meekness. Adopting this stance does wonders for such a leader's ego when, deliberately or otherwise, he does not get the honor or status he deserves. His emotional nurturing comes from his awareness that he is succeeding to some degree in what matters most—the imitation of Christ.

Related to the foregoing teaching is the determination to make *a substantial investment of time, energy, and ability in a God-given calling* without indulging the nagging regret that better use could have been made of these personal resources. Some of the most brilliant and gifted Christian leaders I have been privileged to know have joyously given themselves to their tasks and in the process have characterized themselves as being extraordinarily fortunate or blessed. I suggest these are the meek who are validating their right to inherit the earth or, put another way, to be entrusted with a valuable and extensive heritage.

In summary, *the meek person is God-centered rather than self-centered, committed to service rather than success, and investing in the eternal rather than the temporal.* And he has become this way because he has responded to our Savior's invitation: "Take my yoke upon you and learn from me . . ." (Matthew 11:29).

Judgment Tempered by Goodness

Despite the Lord's judgment of Moses for his failure to be meek at all times, the goodness of the Lord toward Moses above and beyond what might have been expected is highlighted in a New Testament reference.

After six days Jesus took with him Peter, James and John the brother of James, and led them up a high mountain by themselves. There he was transfigured before them. His face shone like the sun, and his clothes became as white as the light. Just then there appeared before them Moses and Elijah, talking with Jesus. (Matthew 17:1-3)

At the time of this event Jesus and the three disciples were in the Promised Land. Thus even though God did not let Moses go there with His people, He graciously let him enter it on the Mount of Transfiguration that day, to talk with the Lord Jesus and with Elijah. In speculation on my part, I imagine that Moses might have told the Lord how much he appreciated this experience, after he had centuries earlier so lost his temper and dishonored the Lord's name that he deserved his punishment of having to stay on the other side of the Jordan. Yet now Moses had the privilege of entering the land and even having a conversation with God's incarnate Son.

Some conclusions may be drawn from this incident. Our shortcomings necessarily and properly bring God's punishment, but He still is merciful and gracious. When we see His entire plan for us, we will be moved by an overwhelming sense of gratitude. We will find that not only is God just, but He is also generous and merciful, far beyond what we deserve.

This incident also says something to us about the use or misuses of whatever strengths we have. Over the years I have watched a number of very gifted Christian leaders begin an enterprise and then later resign or be replaced. While the dynamics of these situations are often complex and are influenced by external as well as internal forces, I propose a generalization that describes some leaders well: their strengths are also their weaknesses. Let me explain.

Getting a pioneer work started requires a great deal of determination and fixed purpose. Otherwise the project would be abandoned because the obstacles, to an ordinary person, would seem insurmountable. But the tenacity that was necessary at the outset can later be an inflexible and arbitrary stance that brooks no challenge and sees no validity in another perspective.

Or an individual may be just the right person to effect healing and reconciliation in an organization fractured by the leadership just described. But then the kind and gentle person turns out to be incapable of making hard decisions or acting forthrightly when a crisis arrives. Instead, he prefers to leave town or to hope that someone else will intervene while he preserves his reputation of sweet reasonableness.

In Moses' case his ability to become justly angry was constructive when he came down from the mountain and judged the people, but this ability to respond quickly to a situation was misused at the waters of Meribah.

Some leaders are adept at developing a consensus and rightly seek to have the group feel a sense of ownership. But when the best efforts fail to bring about agreement and a deadline for a decision has been reached, these leaders too often prefer to be liked rather than to be decisive in doing the right but unpopular thing. We have also known leaders who were indiscriminately generous and then left their successors a monumental deficit. Or we recall tight-fisted administrators who always have a financial surplus but a negative balance of met needs.

Fortunate indeed is the Christian leader who has taken seriously the dictum "Know thyself" and builds on his strengths and accepts his limitations. The grieving David, mourning the death of Absalom, needed a Joab to counterbalance his understandable emotional excesses and so preserve the kingdom (2 Samuel 19:1-8). Similarly Moses, the imaginative and inspiring strategist and spokesman for God, needed to extricate himself from his fascination with administrative detail (Exodus 18:13-26). Far less admirable was David's effort to preserve a reputation for magnanimity and delegate to Solomon the punitive judgment he really had in mind (1 Kings 2:8-10), such as the execution of Joab because of his murders of Abner and Amasa (two of Israel's commanders) and the death of Shimei because he cursed David when he fled from his son Absalom.

In summary, it is necessary to identify and to exercise the strengths God gives us, but it is also realistic and prudent to discern when these strengths may need to be counterbalanced by other individuals committed to the same cause and gifted in complementary ways.

This same quality of leadership may be expected of groups of believers as well as individuals. One of the reasons the Lord sovereignly revealed the vision of the seven churches to John at Patmos was to have these various congregations be examples, whether positively or negatively. An examination of chapters 2 and 3 of the book of Revelation will disclose both what is and what ought to be in the life and ministry of congregations and, by extension, of Christian organizations in general.

Also evident in the account is the role of circumstances in the life of these churches. The Bible teaches that God uses circumstances constructively to challenge us and to make evident those aspects of our lives that need improvement or change. Surely this was true of Moses. And so it is with congregations or Christian organizations. Those that are inordinately self-assured need to learn to depend on the Lord. Those that are unduly preoccupied need to review their priorities. And those that have lost their sense of vision and calling need to become aware of the perilous position they are in.

But why has God expressed this concern? He wanted groups of Christians down the centuries to have a Biblical model. The church in China, for example, in the latter part of the twentieth century needed this Biblical model and became an inspiring example of spiritual fidelity and devotion for those in the West.

Christian leaders, then, not only should be models or patterns of dynamic, Spirit-directed individuals, but also should cultivate in those groups they lead the Biblical qualities exhibited by congregations faithful to Scriptural imperatives.

No doubt Moses made a profound impression on Joshua, his close companion in leadership. And surely the book of Deuteronomy was Moses' final, eloquent effort to summon Israel to be committed to Biblical commands. We do well to learn from this outstanding leader—a truly meek man.

12

Rationalizing

He [Saul] waited seven days, the time set by Samuel; but Samuel did not come to Gilgal, and Saul's men began to scatter. So he said, "Bring me the burnt offering and the fellowship offerings." And Saul offered up the burnt offering. Just as he finished making the offering, Samuel arrived, and Saul went out to greet him. "What have you done?" asked Samuel. Saul replied, "When I saw that the men were scattering, and that you did not come at the set time, and that the Philistines were assembling at Micmash, I thought, 'Now the Philistines will come down against me at Gilgal, and I have not sought the Lord's favor.' So I felt compelled to offer the burnt offering." (1 Samuel 13:8-12)

For a man with Saul's natural and supernatural endowments to fail miserably appears surprising initially. Though chosen to be Israel's first king, he did not seek the monarchy. Yet Saul was an impressive man with kingly credentials. Some of his qualifications are spelled out in chapters 9 and 10 of 1 Samuel. For one thing, he was tall and handsome. Ronald Knox translates 1 Samuel 9:2 in an interesting way: "a fine figure of a man, none finer in Israel." Quite possibly he looked like one of our rugged, attractive athletes—a man's man.

Despite his good looks, Saul was modest. He accepted the fact that his family was not well-known or prominent in Israel. And when searchers tried to find him to make him king, Saul was hiding among the baggage. This self-effacing may be one reason God looked upon him with favor and was willing to equip him for the monarchy.

From chapter 10 we know that God had endowed Saul supernaturally as well as naturally, for Scripture says, "God changed Saul's heart" (v. 9). Furthermore, he was privileged to have associates who also were blessed by God: "Saul went . . . accompanied by valiant men whose hearts God had touched" (v. 26).

Early in his reign Saul showed uncommon charity. Some had objected to his becoming king; yet when he experienced his first triumph and was urged to be vindictive, Saul's reply was, "No one shall be put to death today, for this day the Lord has rescued Israel" (11:13). The fact, then, that Saul had substantial natural and supernatural endowments makes all the more significant the record of his reign—and his fall.

Several key factors determined Saul's course of action and his ultimate downfall. All who have the responsibilities of leadership should note these factors well, for in principle they are yet today issues to be faced.

Expediency Leads to Disobedience

The Scriptural passage cited at the beginning of this chapter describes how Saul, on the basis of expediency, was willing to disobey a Biblical principle. Obviously he knew that only the priests of the Lord were to offer sacrifices and that he, being of the tribe of Benjamin, was not eligible to do so. Yet he permitted the crisis of the moment to dominate him to such an extent that he became willing to violate the Law of God. He was persuaded that the circumstances justified the violation.

Rationalization of this sort would today be called *situation ethics*. Those who espouse this position argue that while a Biblical commandment may apply in a majority of cases, there can be exceptions. For example, sexual immorality may be wrong, they admit, but if such action results in personal fulfillment, it is justified. God, of course, finds such thought abhorrent.

Sadly, this type of rationalization is not absent from Christian circles. Some years ago a man spoke at Wheaton College in one of our gatherings. At that time of year relatively few people attended. Later a public relations agency that was doing some work for the individual wrote to ask for a photograph of the occasion at which he had spoken. We sent the photograph. A few days later the agency returned the print with a notation that it was unacceptable. They asked that instead we furnish them with a picture of the auditorium filled with people. We declined.

In their enthusiasm to build the image of their client, they apparently assumed he would be more used of God if the public got the impression that he had spoken to an overflow crowd. In this case truthfulness was less important than the reputation of their client. I suspect that the man himself was not aware of his agency's practices, but the incident illustrates the tendency even among Christians to base actions on contrivances rather than on principles.

Scripture indicates this was Saul's point of view. He was governed by expediency in reaction to circumstances.

"Just as he finished making the offering, Samuel arrived. . . . 'What have you done?' asked Samuel" (13:10, 11). Saul must have been astonished that immediately after he had offered the sacrifice, Samuel came. God frequently tests us in this way. The lesson is clear: when we are tempted to set aside a commandment of God to do something that is expedient, we must not do it.

My wife and I used to make frequent trips to Chicago's O'Hare Airport. Often it seemed as if some little creature went before us turning the traffic lights red all along the way, particularly when we had left later than we should have. If no one was coming, the temptation was to go through despite the red signal. We could have rationalized such behavior by arguing that we had to get to the airport before take-off, especially since I was on a mission for the Lord.

But then, once we had resisted the temptation and had driven under pressure, we would arrive only to find that the flight had been delayed. I could almost hear the Lord gently saying, "I knew it all the time. Why didn't you trust Me instead of getting so upset?"

Had I gone through red lights, broken the law, tried to justify my behavior, and then found my disobedience was needless, I would have been forced to conclude that being governed by the circumstances of the moment was unjustified. (We should note, however, that even if the disobedience does seem to work out favorably, it is still wrong and will be judged by God.)

In Saul's case, he capitulated to taking the quickest and seemingly most justified course of action. Yet in another few minutes he could have seen God's answer to his need in the coming of Samuel. How much better it would have been had Saul refused to be controlled by circumstances but instead had held fast to what he knew was right.

Unreasonable Leaders Skew Programs

Another significant factor contributing to Saul's failure as a leader was his propensity for being impulsive and arbitrary. First Samuel 14 tells the story. Jonathan and his armor-bearer attacked the enemy and defeated them. All the people, gathered together for battle, were hungry. But Saul had issued a command: "'Cursed be any man who eats food before evening comes, before I have avenged myself on my enemies!' So none of the troops tasted food" (v. 24).

Jonathan, not having heard the command, saw some honey and ate a little of it. As a result, he gained some quick energy and felt reinvigorated. But someone told his father, and this precipitated a crisis. Saul announced to Jonathan he would have to die because he had broken the king's commandment. Outraged by what they perceived to be an unfair judgment, the people prevented Saul from carrying out his threat. The effect of this showdown became evident later.

An important lesson can be drawn from this event. Occasionally a leader will give a directive that is unreasonable, even denying his subordinates the means to do their job. In desperation people may then take things into their own hands. That is what happened here: "They pounced on the plunder and, taking sheep, cattle and calves, they butchered them on the ground and ate them, together with the blood" (v. 32). The Israelites knew it was a sin to eat the blood, but they were too hungry and demoralized to care.

Be assured that if you establish regulations which deny people the tools and the freedom to do their work, they will find a way to meet their need, even if it means doing it in the wrong way.

I know of organizations that pay their employees less than they should—scarcely a living wage. As a result, their employees find it necessary to take supplementary jobs in order to meet their obligations. When these individuals are asked why they were not on hand when they were needed for some special task, they try to evade the issue by saying they just were not available. The fact is, they were occupied elsewhere. Not being paid enough, they found another way to meet their need, even though the method used worked against their commitment to the organization. How much better it is to pay a living wage and have people giving full measure than to have them tired, preoccupied, or even serving only part-time.

Another form of deprivation, so to speak, is for some organizations to pay little heed to the suggestions of their employees and in fact to impose restrictions on their criticisms. You know what happens. The criticism continues. The talk goes on. But opinions are verbalized in the wrong places, usually producing distrust, alienation, and disloyalty, reactions that are really counter to what God's Word teaches. The man at the top may think everything is fine until conditions reach a crisis. How much better to be less arbitrary and to be more reasonable in order to provide legitimate ways for the expression of opinions!

Christian leaders can learn from Saul's mistake of issuing an arbitrary and unreasonable command that led the people to disobey God by eating blood. If we profit from his mistake, we may avoid the problem that developed out of his error and facilitate rather than inhibit obedience to Biblical commands.

Obedience Must Be Total

A third factor causing Saul's downfall was his incomplete obedience when he was ordered to destroy the Amalekites and all they had. The Scripture describes Samuel's confrontation of Saul:

> Early in the morning Samuel got up and went to meet Saul, but he was told, "Saul has gone to Carmel. There he has set up a monument in his own honor and has turned and gone on down to Gilgal." When Samuel reached him, Saul said, "The Lord bless you! I have carried out the Lord's instructions." But Samuel said, "What is this bleating of sheep in my ears? What then is this lowing of cattle that I hear?" (15:12-14)

Disobedience makes fools out of us. What Saul said was obviously untrue. How could he possibly claim to have followed the commandment of the Lord? Yet when Saul was disobedient, he became fearful; and to defend himself, he voiced things that were ridiculous.

Now let us return to the Biblical narrative. "Saul answered, 'The soldiers brought them from the Amalekites; they spared the best of the sheep and cattle to sacrifice to the Lord your God'" (v. 15). Note the reasoning. The justification for disobeying God was to obtain materials with which to worship the Lord. This would be akin to stealing money to give to God.

What was Samuel's response to Saul's pitiful attempt to cover his disobedience? Samuel reminded Saul that the Lord had chosen him when he was unknown, had made him king, and had empowered him to destroy his enemies. "Why did you not obey the Lord? Why did you pounce on the plunder and do evil in the eyes of the Lord?" (v. 19). Notice Saul's reply and then Samuel's rejoinder:

> "But I did obey the Lord," Saul said. "I went on the mission the Lord assigned me. I completely destroyed the Amalekites and brought back Agag their king. The soldiers took sheep and cattle from the plunder, the best of what was devoted to God, in order to sacrifice them to the Lord your God at Gilgal." (vv. 20, 21)

> But Samuel replied: "Does the Lord delight in burnt offerings and sacrifices as much as in obeying the voice of the Lord? To obey is better than sacrifice, and to heed is better than the fat of rams. For rebellion is like the sin of divination, and arrogance like the evil of idolatry. Because you have rejected the word of the Lord, he has rejected you as king." (vv. 22, 23)

In light of Samuel's deep feeling for Saul (see 1 Samuel 15:35), I imagine that he spoke these words with a trembling voice and with tears in his eyes. In any event, Saul at last acknowledged his sin. He confessed to Samuel, "I have sinned. I violated the Lord's command and your instructions. I was afraid of the people and so I gave in to them" (v. 24).

I suspect that the people were wary of Saul. After all, they had recently, because of an unjustified restriction, taken things into their own hands and had refused to let Saul execute Jonathan. I suppose they resolved next time they went out to battle and there was spoil to take, they were not going to get caught short again. In case the king made another arbitrary decision not to take spoil, they were going to get as much as they could before he issued such an order.

I am reminded with some chagrin of a certain behavior in my

Navy days. When we went ashore, we would go over the gangway and onto the dock and then run as fast as we could for the gate. We had a reason for our haste. Sometimes when we were all set to go ashore and had already received permission to leave the ship, we were told we had to stay aboard to supervise the loading of ammunition or to do some other task. We would think about all those who had already left while we were faced with the tasks that had kept us from leaving. You can imagine what we were pondering: "The next time we plan to go ashore, we'll get on that dock and run for the gate and get away before any announcement to remain on board is made."

I am embarrassed at the way we ran for the gate. But it was a natural reaction to being kept aboard when many others had gone ashore. I think this was the attitude of the people under Saul. Since they were needlessly denied food the previous time, now they were going to take whatever they could get. The result was that the king, who had prompted this reaction by his overly arbitrary restrictions, lost the confidence of his subjects and eventually failed to lead them as he should.

Saul was partly right when he said the soldiers had taken the animals, but Scripture records (15:9) that he joined them in this. Was he unsure he could restrain them? But he was the king and was accountable for what they did. Anyone in a responsible position may on occasion permit subordinates to act independently, or even follow their proposals, but the leader is still accountable for what happens and cannot shift the blame to his subordinates. That is the price of leadership.

Indeed, leaders should take responsibility even for actions resulting from disobedience, as Moses did in pleading with the Lord for rebellious Israel (Exodus 32:11-13).

The Deterioration of Leadership Continues

One more incident, when taken with the others, depicts a pattern of deterioration which I believe is not only chronological but logical.

First came expediency in place of principle. A reaction to that expediency resulted in an arbitrariness that went to the other extreme. The ensuing loss of confidence and control led to putting unjustified blame on subordinates. Finally, as 1 Samuel 28:5-25 carefully details, Saul could no longer sense the Lord's presence and therefore determined to call up Samuel from the grave for instructions on fighting the Philistines.

Psalm 66:18 says, "If I had cherished sin in my heart, the Lord would not have listened." I believe Saul's behavior pattern during the last years of his reign gives evidence that his disobedience to God continued; so God no longer listened. Saul inexorably progressed to the place where he was not only discredited among his people, but was also unable to receive the guidance, wisdom, and enablement he needed from the Lord.

The lesson to be learned from the tragic life of Saul is sobering. Once principle is ignored in favor of expediency, and expediency justifies arbitrary directives, one comes across as unpredictable and driven by circumstances rather than convictions. It is then tempting to shift the blame to others as if one's decisions were simply governed by consensus. The combination of disobedience and abdication results in a loss of God's fellowship and consequently of God's wisdom and power. In such a state it is difficult both emotionally and spiritually to act coherently. The result is frustration and futility.

Some of the recent failures of religious leaders seem to have their cause in behavior patterns similar to Saul's. By insisting that they knew God's will better than the historic agreement on the meaning of Scripture, and then arbitrarily imposing a program that clearly lacked justification, followed by an assignment of blame to the people of God if the resulting crises were not resolved, they employed that which caused Saul's problems and theirs as well.

After six years as president of Ohio's Antioch College, Dr. Douglas McGregor commented in an address, "The Boss Must Be Boss":

I believed a leader could operate successfully as a kind of advisor . . . avoid being a boss. Unconsciously, I suspect, I hoped to duck the unpleasant necessity of making difficult decisions, of taking the responsibility for one course of action among many uncertain alternatives, of making mistakes and taking the consequences. . . . I couldn't have been more wrong. It took a couple of years, but I finally began to realize that a leader cannot avoid the exercise of authority any more than he can avoid responsibility for what happens to his organization.

Saul provides a vivid illustration of one who needs to learn what Dr. McGregor found by experience to be true. It is regrettable that we need to relearn what is already documented in Scripture. That really is the focus of this chapter: we can avoid repeating the mistakes of the past and reaping their inevitable devastating harvest. If the Bible is the only infallible rule of faith and practice—and it is—we can gain both insight and application from Saul's experience.

It is well to recognize, however, that the serpent's luring question in the Garden of Eden, "Did God really say?," persists in the thinking of even those located within the believing community. I find it noteworthy that the Bible is filled with exhortations and warnings and pathetic examples, such as that of Saul, for the instruction of God's people. Clearly, He knows of our proclivity to question or to ignore His pronouncements, and He loves us too much to abandon us to our own devices.

Thus, while we may have a multitude of societal examples to the contrary ("Everybody's doing it"), we are responsible to be informed and then to be obedient. May we allow the Biblical conformity of our lives to manifest the illumination of Holy Scripture and the enablement of the Holy Spirit. Then, like Saul's successor David, we can be those "after his [God's] own heart" (1 Samuel 13:14).

13

Handling Success

J. B. Phillips, the famed translator and essayist, entitled his autobiography *The Price of Success*. An eloquent passage explains why:

I was in a state of some excitement throughout the whole of 1955. My work hardly seemed arduous for it was intrinsically exciting. I was tasting the sweets of success to an almost unimaginable degree; my health was excellent; my future prospects were rosier than my wildest dreams could ever suggest; applause, honour and appreciation met me wherever I went. I was well aware of the dangers of sudden wealth and I took some severe measures to make sure that, although comfortable, I should never be rich. I was not nearly so aware of the dangers of success. The subtle corrosion of character, the unconscious changing of values and the secret monstrous growth of a vastly inflated idea of myself seeped slowly into me. Vaguely I was aware of this and, like some frightful parody of St. Augustine, I prayed, "Lord, make me humble—but not yet." I can still savour the sweet and gorgeous taste of it all—the warm admiration, the sense of power, of overwhelming ability, of boundless energy and never failing enthusiasm.

And then Phillips concludes,

It is very plain to me now why my one man kingdom of power and glory had to stop.

One of the most formidable tests a leader must face is success, especially when his record of faithfulness in itself is most commendable. King Hezekiah was confronted with just such a challenge. He had been unusually faithful in his reign as king over God's people, but when he put confidence in himself rather than in God, he learned just how inadequate such misplaced trust can be.

Poor Family Background

Hezekiah's background varied considerably from that of Solomon. We see a description of Hezekiah's father in 2 Kings 16:2—"Ahaz was twenty years old when he became king, and he reigned in Jerusalem sixteen years. Unlike David his father, he did not do what was right in the eyes of the Lord his God."

Although having a faithless father is a liability, it is a mistake to think that the only way to be a success is to have a proper background. Had he lived in our day, Hezekiah might very well have been perceived as having only a marginal chance of becoming a leader of integrity. Many would assume that he would not possess high moral and ethical qualities because his parental influence was so bad. Hezekiah dramatically refuted that notion.

Such an example does not invalidate parental responsibility to provide a good background, but it does suggest that children are to be personally accountable as they grow up. Hezekiah stands as an inspiring model of one who rose above his parental influence to become a man of God.

Taking Initiative Early

When he came to the throne at the age of twenty-five, Hezekiah immediately instituted a series of reforms. His decisiveness led to the reestablishment of Temple worship. People had resorted to alternate practices resulting in a religious syncretism—a mixing of contradictory faiths.

Some years ago my father visited Central America and brought back a photograph of a church. In the foreground a fire was burning. My father learned that the religious people who came to that community years before had built the church to counteract the worship of the Fire God. So a church was constructed in the same location where these rites were held. But instead of making a clear distinction between the two forms of religion, the people developed a syncretism. They would come to the entrance of the church and build a fire to worship the Fire God and then proceed into the church in an effort to obtain the best of both religious systems.

To avoid such unacceptable practices, Hezekiah recognized it would be necessary to establish the kind of worship that had been commanded by the Lord God. Further, he realized that the Temple would be its focal point. At the same time, it would be necessary to abolish all other forms of worship.

Hezekiah's strong leadership was also evidenced in his restoration of Passover, a ceremony which reminded God's people of one of the great events connected with their emancipation centuries earlier. Through celebrating the Passover, the people focused on their deliverance from the bondage of Egypt into the liberty of the Promised Land. Thus Hezekiah, with a perspective that was both Scriptural and historical, summoned the people to celebrate the Passover, even asking those from beyond the borders of his kingdom to join with them in the remembrance at Jerusalem. And his effort proved successful.

Hezekiah's example remains instructive now. Currently some of the major events which brought the church to where it is today are suspect because they are viewed as embarrassing or anachronistic. For example, one hears little about the Reformation as we each year come to October 31, the date on which Martin Luther posted his Ninety-five Theses. As a convinced Protestant, I have concluded that certain important truths were recovered at the Reformation—truths that are central to what we believe today: Scripture alone, faith alone, grace alone, and direct access to the presence of the Lord. An annual emphasis of these points is in order. I have discovered, however, a reluctance by many to highlight the Reformation or to include it on the Christian calendar.

Let me suggest some possible reasons. The stress being placed upon personal relationships renders the concept of salvation for some as little more than the experience of a dynamic encounter rather than an act of God's grace received by faith alone. Furthermore, the functions of the gathered church tend increasingly to reflect current cultural ideas rather than divine imperatives. For these reasons we need specific times and places to rejoice in the acts of God—as, for example, in the Reformation—and to make these part of our heritage.

Success on Every Front

Success followed success for Hezekiah. He triumphed in military affairs as well as in spiritual ones. Sennacherib's troops had come to the gate of the city. The Assyrian king's representative, Rab-shakeh, threatened the Jews on the wall, using their own language. Realizing the critical nature of the situation, Hezekiah committed the entire matter to the Lord, acknowledging his need of divine help and praying that in it all God would be glorified. In response the Lord delivered Hezekiah and his people, giving them a tremendous victory. No doubt Hezekiah was thereafter perceived as a man of extraordinary faith.

The Problem of Success

But after his accomplishments, based on commendable convictions, Hezekiah in time came to face what I call the problem of success. From his experience we can learn that a leader with an outstanding record and Biblical convictions may be vulnerable to the temptations that success brings.

Just when Hezekiah was feeling invincible and indispensable, he faced the supreme crisis of his life.

> In those days Hezekiah became ill and was at the point of death. The prophet Isaiah son of Amoz went to him and said, "This is what the Lord says: Put your house in order, because you will die; you will not recover." Hezekiah turned his face to the wall and prayed to the Lord, "Remember, O Lord, how I have walked before you faithfully and with wholehearted devotion and have done what is good in your eyes." And Hezekiah wept bitterly. (2 Kings 20:1-3)

Had I been Hezekiah at thirty-nine years of age, I suspect I too would have had some deep feelings. I might have said, "Lord, since my life is just beginning to be productive, under Your good hand, isn't my imminent death premature?" In somewhat the same spirit Hezekiah rehearsed to the Lord all that he had done (this is also described in Isaiah 38:2, 3).

An Importunate Prayer

Hezekiah pled so fervently for his life that God granted him additional years.

> Before Isaiah had left the middle court, the word of the Lord came to him: "Go back and tell Hezekiah . . . 'I have heard your prayer and seen your tears; I will heal you . . . I will add fifteen years to your life. . . .'" (vv. 4-6)

This importunate request of Hezekiah for additional years reminds me of a verse that some years ago struck me with great force as I read it in the *King James Version*. Although Psalm 106:15 is talking about the nation of Israel rather than an individual, the principle applies individually as well as collectively:

And he gave them their request; but sent leanness into their soul.

Sometimes I have heard people say in their prayers, "God, You just have to do this." And in fact at times when individuals have demanded that their request be granted, things turned out that way. Some might conclude this is the manner by which to approach God—to insist upon having one's request. But this verse of Scripture suggests that our longed-for results may not be favorable.

Others criticize the use of the phrase "If it be God's will," viewing it as a kind of escape mechanism, so that no matter what happens, it can be said God had His way. Yet a sublime example in the use of "if it be Your will" is found in Jesus' prayer in Gethsemane: "Father, if you are willing, take this cup from me; yet not my will, but yours be done" (Luke 22:42). I am prepared to follow the example of our Lord Jesus Christ. Otherwise God may grant my request but send leanness into my soul.

Some couples have acknowledged that they were called of God to serve on the mission field, only to begin thinking about all the reasons which might preclude their going. They wondered if later on they would be unable to provide an education for their children. They became concerned about their health needs. They questioned whether or not they could find a proper outlet for the abilities God had given them. So they said to the Lord, "We insist that we stay home." And they did so.

But now, in middle age, a number of these individuals experience an emptiness of life and a sense of futility. Now they wish they had not demanded their own way, but rather had been willing to accept the will of God for them.

The objection might be raised that submission to God's will may be all well and good when the issue has to do simply with one option or another in our ministry, but when one's life is at stake, it is only natural to plead with God to be able to live a little longer. Here the experience of Hezekiah becomes particularly instructive. He had been unusually successful in faith and action. Would he now continue to live to the glory of God if he were allowed to stay on this earth a few years longer?

A Proud Heart

Sadly Scripture tells us that Hezekiah had a change of heart after his healing. "But Hezekiah's heart was proud and he did not respond to the kindness shown him" (2 Chronicles 32:25).

In crying out to God asking to be healed, Hezekiah thought only about saving his life. But God knew that when Hezekiah was healed, rather than giving glory to the Lord he would become proud and would boast about his healing. Furthermore, since he had been guaranteed fifteen more years of life, perhaps this made him less committed to the obedient stewardship of each day, despite what he said in Isaiah 38:10-20 just after he was healed.

How would you and I react if we were granted added years of life? We might well reason that we would have ample time to do this or that. Thus the years would slip by swiftly while we procrastinated. Whether or not this was Hezekiah's problem, it became clear that he could not handle the success and blessing which had been given him. I believe God foresaw this problem and suggest that an earlier homegoing would have saved Hezekiah from doing what later discredited him.

Hezekiah's attitude of pride is depicted in what he did when emissaries from Babylon came to visit him:

> Hezekiah received the messengers and showed them all that was in his storehouses. . . . There was nothing in his palace or in all his kingdom that Hezekiah did not show them.
> Then Isaiah the prophet went to King Hezekiah and asked . . . "What did they see in your palace?" . . . "everything . . ." Hezekiah said. . . . Then Isaiah said to Hezekiah, "Hear the word of the Lord: The time will surely come when everything

in your palace . . . will be carried off to Babylon." (2 Kings 20:13-17)

We may infer from this passage and from Isaiah's rebuke that Hezekiah took pride in all of these things as if they were his own possessions rather than what he held in stewardship for the Lord. God in His omniscience knew that Hezekiah, if he were spared, would not only glory in the act of healing rather than in the Healer, but also would become preoccupied with the wealth of his kingdom rather than with the Giver of all these things. Thus Hezekiah turned from the Blesser to the blessings.

When the inexorable progression of a terminal illness, for example, seems to indicate that God has set a time for us to die, we ought to acknowledge that He knows best, even though it is natural for us to cling to life. This is not to suggest that we be presumptuous or refuse to use medical help or fail to be prudent in the way we live. It does mean, however, that we are to trust our sovereign Lord to do the very best for us.

Consider the experience of Paul Little, the Inter-Varsity Christian Fellowship worker who became so well-loved on university campuses. His view of God's sovereignty over his life was included in his last article, published in *Moody Monthly*. In that piece he stated his conviction that God never makes any mistakes. Soon afterward, while Paul was driving south to Toronto, his car went out of control and this gifted man, whose ministry had been a blessing to thousands, was killed.

We could argue that he should have been spared to help his wife and children and to continue his strategic ministry to young people. In bewilderment and almost in despair we might be tempted to ask God, "Why did you take Paul Little at that time?" None of us knows the answer to such a question, but we do know that God does not make any mistakes.

Relying on God's Providence

So whether we die or whether we live, the circumstances of life are not matters of fate but of the providence of God. If He takes us off this earth, God may very well be sparing us or others from something lamentable that we could not know about at the time nor understand until we are in the Lord's presence.

Only in eternity would Hezekiah too realize what could have been avoided had he died at thirty-nine. Although Hezekiah may well have suffered remorse for foolishly showing the treasures of his kingdom to those who were really his enemies, he could not have known that his son Manasseh was to become one of the most wicked and brutal kings ever to reign over Judah. The Biblical account says that Manasseh filled Jerusalem with the blood of his victims. The record of Manasseh's calculated disobedience is repeatedly cited as the cause of God's later judgment on the nation.

The striking statistic is that Manasseh was twelve years old when he succeeded his father on the throne. This son, born during the extension of time given Hezekiah, did irreparable harm to the cause of God's people. We can only surmise that it would have been far better for Hezekiah and his kingdom had he died rather than having been granted the additional fifteen years. God's people would have been spared Manasseh's persecution, bloodshed, and tyranny.

When we demand that God must do it our way, we demonstrate that our perspective does not fit with the Biblical view of life, death, and eternity. Notice how clearly this is illustrated by Hezekiah as recorded in 2 Chronicles 32:31—"But when envoys were sent by the rulers of Babylon to ask him about the miraculous sign that had occurred in the land, God left him to test him and to know everything that was in his heart." When we say to God that He must do what we want, we are proclaiming our judgment to be better than His. In response, God may very well withdraw His informing, protecting, restraining ministry and leave us to ourselves for a time.

We learn, then, that the underlying reasons for Hezekiah's pride and indiscretion in his disclosures to the visitors from Babylon was that God had left him to himself. No doubt it is because he is aware of this principle that Dr. Billy Graham has declared repeatedly throughout his long ministry that if God were to withdraw His hand, Billy's lips would turn to clay. That is not merely a statement for the press. It is the profound conviction of a man who has learned this Biblical lesson and is saying, "Lord, don't leave me to myself, because I already know what is in my heart, and I don't trust my own judgment."

Dealing with Success

For leaders today, Hezekiah is a compelling illustration of one who had strong convictions, great faith, and unusual experiences of deliverance, but who in the final analysis was not prepared to trust God with his entire life. He apparently became too attached to success and to status and to all the good things God had given him.

Realizing that not all Christian leaders—at least at first—are predisposed to recognize and deal with the challenge of success, it is necessary to advance some recommendations in the hope these will prompt a realistic self-appraisal.

A manifest skill in writing or speaking may cause us to reach the false conclusion that perfection in performance automatically develops a degree of personal perfection. Sadly, the opposite is too often the case. In such a situation technique replaces spiritual power and inevitably results in barrenness.

Equally seductive is the invalid assumption that another's dubious success—often quantifiably measured—justifies our pursuing success in the same way, thus questioning whether God really means what He says about unethical behavior. A friend of mine, then in the State Department, told of a colleague's frustration with a missions executive. The colleague saw a fund-raising appeal which represented conditions in an area of the world as requiring immediate help. Yet the State Department official knew these conditions no longer existed.

When he called the missions executive to ask that the misleading appeal be changed, the reply was a refusal since the appeal "made money." Such "success" is really a monumental failure.

Another fallacy is to equate spiritual blessing with growth both in numbers and in scope of ministry. This delusion has on occasion driven Christian leaders to impose a corporate, market-oriented growth pattern on their organization despite obvious personal or organizational limitations. Predictably the outcome goes beyond the capacity of the leadership, finally resulting in what is generally recognized as personal failure.

Part of the problem here may be a matter of focus—on imitation rather than on ministry. The reasoning seems to be that if God has visibly blessed other organizations, even those with questionable practices, surely He would not judge me if I imitate what I have come to admire. Or, if other servants of the Lord celebrate the success of their fund-raising by going "first class," then I should be able to do the same.

Perhaps it is right to ask why we have so many visible cases of affluence and so few visible cases of selfless service—Mother Teresa being one. As best I can determine, Mother Teresa is an example of handling success rather than allowing success to dominate her.

I am impressed by the fact that it is not ignorance of Biblical teachings that causes us to fail here. As Paul says in Philippians 3:16, we should order our lives by what we already know by experience to be right.

Defeat After Success

Hezekiah's example also provides another lesson for those in Christian leadership: God may not ask us to give up our lives, but He may test us just as dramatically as He did Hezekiah by asking us to come to the place where it would be the same as if we had died. That is, we would no longer have our assignment, our resources, our authority, our subordinates.

If all of these were to be withdrawn, would we still trust the Lord? Or would we say that the price is too high and ask to stay in our present situation? The Christian leader may have no idea why he is being asked to withdraw from all the excitement, the blessing, and the challenge of his work, as if God had told him he was going to die. But he must understand that if God asks this of him, he must do the Lord's will or experience serious consequences.

The leader can gain a balanced perspective through an awareness of the Biblical view of success and its significance in the economy of God. Philip's experience as recorded in Acts 8:26-40 provides insight into this matter. Earlier in the chapter the account of Philip's ministry makes clear that it could be described as successful. Crowds came to hear him, and unusual spiritual power was manifested. Suddenly God sent Philip out to a lonely desert road. Scripture is silent as to the evangelist's reaction, but some of us might have been prompted to demur, arguing that the signs of blessing were tangible evidences that the Lord's will was being done. What possibly could be as important as winning converts and bringing great joy to the people?

Perhaps here we have another documentation of the fact that we see in part and are too often provincial in outlook. Thankfully Philip simply started walking and on the way met the Ethiopian eunuch, who received Christ and undoubtedly took the gospel back to his homeland.

We should not conclude that a work will falter and die if we leave. In other words, a work's success and our ministry are not inextricably intertwined. When this delusion prompts us to challenge God's directives or refuse to go, as Jonah did, we have a badly distorted view of success and will falter spiritually.

Similarly, the apparent isolation and lack of opportunity may reinforce our conviction that surely God has not really redirected us. What is striking about this account, however, is that Philip's promptness to obey coincided exactly with the eunuch's travel plans—as the sovereign Lord knew they would.

Yet there may still be the nagging doubt that ministering to one person cannot be as successful as preaching to crowds. What preacher called to a small congregation in a remote area has not wondered what it must be like to be a Luis Palau. But Luis would be the first to affirm that he is but one part of God's strategy of ministry and outreach.

This Biblical illustration, then, underscores the fact that we are not called to be successful but to be *obedient*. Surely the example our Lord Himself sets for us affirms this. Success in the popular meaning of the word would have been achieved if He had come in power and glory and vanquished all His foes. To be sure, He will do this someday, but in His incarnation He chose, we might say, the desert road in order to fit exactly into the divine timetable, the fullness of time. And as Philippians 2:5-11 tells us, it was His obedience that prompted His humiliation and death—hardly success in the popular perception.

I believe Paul too learned this lesson well and then was able to traverse the range of human experience with equanimity. He had learned to be content whatever his current situation (Philippians 4:10-13). No longer was he nourished with applause; he was stabilized and tranquil because he trusted God's sovereignty. So should we.

We should each ask ourselves regularly whether we serve the Lord merely because He blesses us or because He is Lord. J. B. Phillips suffered severe depression and loss of ability as the price of success, but he also learned to give glory to God. Let the most successful of us ponder this fact and recall that "whatever you do, do it all for the glory of God" (1 Corinthians 10:31).

14

Accountability

*The fear of the Lord—that is wisdom, and to shun evil is
understanding.* (Job 28:28)

O h, for the wisdom of Solomon!" one often hears. At times
the complexities and perplexities of Christian work cause
the leader to wish for the intellectual advantages Solomon
enjoyed. But a consideration of Solomon's life makes plain that one
needs more than wisdom if his performance is to please God. Because
of his failure to recognize the principle of accountability, Solomon
stands as one of the most tragic figures in Biblical history.

Blessed from Birth

Solomon had much in his favor when he began his public role as king
of Israel. From his birth he had had the blessing of God upon him.
"The Lord loved him; and because the Lord loved him, he sent word
through Nathan the prophet to name him Jedidiah" (2 Samuel
12:24). The name Jedidiah means "beloved of the Lord." In his very
name Solomon had the assurance that God loved him.

God's blessing extended to Solomon's being selected king from
among David's children. "Then King David said to the whole assem-

bly: 'My son Solomon, the one whom God has chosen, is young and inexperienced . . .'" (1 Chronicles 29:1). While we have no elaboration of this statement, it seems clear that David was persuaded God had led him to designate Solomon as his successor.

Solomon also had the benefit of his father's intercessory prayer, as recorded in 1 Chronicles 29:19—"And give my son Solomon the wholehearted devotion to keep your commands, requirements and decrees and to do everything to build the palatial structure for which I have provided." The fuller text of this prayer is in Psalm 72, where we cannot help being impressed by the petitions David made to God on behalf of his son. He asked for acceptance, blessing, power, and influence for Solomon, and his petitions were granted.

I know something of this kind of blessing from personal experience, for I had godly parents. One of the reasons I have missed my mother during the years she has been with the Lord is because she was faithful in her intercessory ministry for me. I believe I was often preserved morally and spiritually as well as physically because Mother stood in the gap, so to speak, to pray for her son. I thank the Lord for this.

Similarly, I now also miss the daily intercession my father made on my behalf before the Lord. During the long years he was given (nearly ninety-eight) he had an increasingly vital prayer ministry and requested specific blessings upon my life and service. Blessed indeed is a son who has such parents.

While we are not able to demonstrate a direct cause-and-effect relationship, some of the difficulties Solomon encountered may have occurred because David had died and was no longer an intercessor for his son. Of course such ministry is not limited to parents. If you know someone who has become prominent and successful, pray for that person. And urge others to pray for you. Intercessory prayer cannot help but make a difference in undergirding a leader's ministry.

Of course Solomon himself was certainly personally accountable, but he might have done better had he continued to receive the support David had provided during his lifetime. In my case I am blessed to have a praying wife and children and also friends who regularly uphold me before "the throne of grace" (Hebrews 4:16).

It has been suggested that David did not adequately discipline Solomon. There may be a basis for that criticism, though 1 Chronicles 28 indicates David did not limit his parental concern to prayer but charged Solomon explicitly:

> "And you, my son Solomon, acknowledge the God of your father, and serve him with wholehearted devotion and with a willing mind, for the Lord searches every heart and understands every motive behind the thoughts. If you seek him, he will be found by you; but if you forsake him, he will reject you forever. Consider now, for the Lord has chosen you to build a temple as a sanctuary. Be strong and do the work." (vv. 9, 10)

Thus David publicly exhorted Solomon to keep in mind that serving the Lord would bring blessing, but disobeying Him would ensure judgment.

Specific Provisions

In addition to being blessed of God from birth and having a father who prayed for him and who offered strong counsel, Solomon received a special gift from the Lord. Notice 1 Chronicles 29:25— "The Lord highly exalted Solomon in the sight of all Israel and bestowed on him royal splendor such as no king over Israel ever had before." Today too God graciously grants this kind of blessing. When the Lord calls a person to a position of leadership, that individual is in a sense magnified in the sight of the people so he may properly exercise the responsibilities of leadership.

This was true for Moses (see Exodus 7:1—the Lord said, "See, I have made you like God to Pharaoh") and for Joshua (see Joshua 3:7—"And the Lord said to Joshua, 'Today I will begin to exalt you in the eyes of all Israel'") and may be inferred from the obvious respect the early church had for the Apostle Paul as well. I believe this pattern prevails today for those called by God to the ministry of leadership.

Finally, Solomon was singularly blessed when the Lord invited him to ask for whatever he wanted. This well-known encounter reads thus: "That night God appeared to Solomon and said to him, 'Ask for whatever you want me to give you'" (2 Chronicles 1:7). The remarkable thing here is that Solomon did not come to the Lord— the Lord came to Solomon. In our day we do not need such visions; we know from New Testament teachings that God invites us to come and ask at any time. Here, though, Solomon was faced with a decision as to what to request.

I suggest that Solomon's reply issued from his background and experience. David's exhortations and prayers had prepared his mind and heart to ask for wisdom.

How generous is our Lord's reply! ". . . wisdom and knowledge will be given you. And I will also give you wealth, riches and honor, such as no king who was before you ever had and none after you will have" (2 Chronicles 1:12).

Taking note of the special preparation and the specific provisions made for Solomon makes us aware that we also may have particular enduements from the Lord for our tasks. For example, we can receive wisdom by asking for it in accordance with God's promise: "If any of you lacks wisdom, he should ask God, who gives generously to all without finding fault, and it will be given to him. But when he asks, he must believe and not doubt" (James 1:5, 6).

Success and Accountability Linked

Despite his extraordinary wisdom, Solomon failed to recognize he was accountable for the resources and prestige God had given to him. He faced tests which modern man also encounters. Scripture describes the way Solomon handled wealth. Notice the interesting contrast in 1 Kings 6:37 and 7:1:

> The foundation of the temple of the Lord was laid in the fourth year, in the month of Ziv. In the eleventh year in the month of Bul, the eighth month, the temple was finished in all its details according to its specifications. He had spent seven years building it. . . . It took Solomon thirteen years, however, to complete the construction of his palace.

We recognize that David had made preparation for the building of the Lord's house by accumulating materials in abundance. We can surmise, therefore, that Solomon could build without delay. Even so, there was a substantial difference between the seven years to build the Lord's house and the thirteen years to construct Solomon's.

Reading about the dimensions and furnishings of Solomon's home suggests that as the construction continued, this man was not interested simply in shelter but in status. While Solomon was faithful in building the Temple of the Lord and establishing it as a place of worship, he was more interested in the building of his own house. The attraction of material things had so penetrated Solomon's consciousness that his priorities were out of order.

You may be pondering, "How can I determine how much money to commit to goods and services I need as compared to what I should designate to the work of the Lord?" Without trying to evade the question, I believe there is no simple, uncomplicated formula to follow. However, two passages in the New Testament, while not dealing specifically with material things, do offer guidance for matters of discretion in which there is no explicit moral or ethical pronouncement.

Romans 14 and 1 Corinthians 8 discuss the question of eating meat offered to idols and of keeping a particular day holy. The principle underlying both passages is that each individual must make an examined decision whether or not to eat meat and whether or not to observe a certain day. Similarly, each of us must make examined decisions about the allocation of our money.

In the 1960s some young people declared, often with great heat, that if a man had more than one suit jacket, he was out of the will of God. These individuals also made a practice of quoting the last part of Acts 4, which says in part that the church had all things in common (v. 32). Even today certain groups of Christians have agreed to pool their resources and live in austerity. I respect their decisions but do not think every Christian must necessarily follow such a manner of life. Let me explain.

Peter, in the opening portion of Acts 5, told Ananias and Sapphira that the land in question was in fact theirs, and when they sold it the proceeds were to be used at their discretion. Had it been an absolute that everyone *had* to sell his land and give all to the church, Peter would have said so. Instead, there was opportunity for personal choice and conviction. Christians could keep their land if the Lord led them to do so, or they could sell it. What was determinative was God's sovereign purpose. And once the land was sold, the owners could give away all the proceeds or just a portion. That was between the principals involved and the Lord.

So with respect to things material, we should not insist that every Christian fit into exactly the same mold. We should also beware of falling prey to "keeping up with the Joneses." If they buy a new automobile, must we buy one? If they add on to their house, should we? If they own a boat and a house in the country, must we? We need not be caught in a tide of steadily rising expectations. Rather, let us make an examined decision based upon whether or not an expenditure will enable us better to perform our ministry.

For example, one might question spending an appreciable sum on air conditioning. Is this expenditure solely for personal comfort or for more effective fulfillment of one's God-given role in life? How much money should a leader allocate for clothing? The issue, of course, is whether or not what we wear is contributing to effective ministry.

When I was ranching in West Texas, I did not wear a suit and tie on the range. Instead, I wore blue jeans, boots, and a western hat. Appearance depends on the circumstances. Out on the ranch I looked like a rancher; before a group of business executives I looked like a college president. In the latter instance, expenditure for a well-fitting suit is justified and to be preferred to wearing something that calls undue attention to oneself.

I recognize that some Christians justify their dress as a sign of poverty and obedience. Yet such observance can sometimes make the wearer an exhibitionist. Whatever your decision in this matter, let it be a calculated one, after prayer. Furthermore, we should recognize that prudence need not trap us in a false economics in which minimal savings are more than offset by unsatisfactory results from the money spent or the needless misuse of time and energy. Let it also be said that our primary goal is service, not savings, and certainly not extravagance.

Scripture offers no indication that Solomon used his extraordinary wisdom to ascertain whether or not he needed all the opulence with which he surrounded himself. To me, it appears that he had gone far beyond the point of necessity even for a king. He could not justify what was really excess and apparently did not even raise the question.

We can all learn from Solomon's experience. May we scrutinize our budgets regularly. If before the Lord we are persuaded we should or should not have a particular building or vehicle or item of clothing, other Christians should respect our choice and not doubt our integrity. But let us take care that each decision is a thoughtful one and that it takes into account that having more things requires more care and attention, which is not always justified. This principle of accountability is integral to our entire ministry of example.

Yielding to Lust

Not only was Solomon enticed by his wealth, but he was lured into flagrant and forbidden sexual excesses.

King Solomon . . . loved many foreign women . . . from nations about which the Lord had told the Israelites, "You must not intermarry with them, because they will surely turn your hearts after their gods." Nevertheless, Solomon held fast to them in love. He had seven hundred wives . . . and three hundred concubines, and his wives led him astray. As Solomon grew old, his wives turned his heart after other gods. . . . So Solomon did evil in the eyes of the Lord. . . . (1 Kings 11:1-6)

Keep in mind that this is the action of the wisest man who ever lived, the man who understood clearly the text and meaning of Holy Scripture and who in writing the book of Proverbs pointed out the pitfalls of sexual lust. Obviously his wisdom was not enough.

I am reminded of an incident that occurred when my wife and I were first married and on our way to San Pedro, California, where my ship was in dry dock. We were traveling by train, in a sleeping car of the type that had curtains to provide privacy for the upper and lower berths.

After my wife and I had gone to bed, we heard a conversation through the curtain. The porter was talking to a young lady. She had come down the aisle to the place just opposite us, where a young military officer had his berth. She was about to enter that berth with him when the porter pleaded, "Miss, you know this is wrong. Please don't do it." I shall always remember her response. She said, "I know it's wrong, but I am going to do it anyway." And she did.

From what Solomon wrote in Proverbs and read in Deuteronomy 17 he too knew that his sexual life was wrong, but pride and lust had so gripped him that he simply would not turn aside from certain sin. Ostentation (having many wives) and the resulting sexual license had become a preoccupation with him, and he was not about to give up his manner of life. In so doing he ignored the exhortations from God Himself, who warned Solomon about the consequences of disobedience.

... the Lord appeared to him a second time. ... The Lord said to him: ... "if you walk before me in integrity of heart and uprightness, as David your father did, and do all I command and observe my decrees and laws, I will establish your royal throne over Israel forever. ... But if you or your sons turn away from me and do not observe the commands and decrees I have given you and go off to serve other gods and worship them, then I will cut off Israel from the land I have given them and will reject this temple. ... Israel will then become a byword and an object of ridicule among all peoples." (1 Kings 9:1-7)

A later remonstrance is recorded in 1 Kings 11:

So the Lord said to Solomon, "Since this is your attitude and you have not kept my covenant and my decrees, which I commanded you, I will most certainly tear the kingdom away from you and give it to one of your subordinates." (v. 11)

Notice how persistently God acted to dissuade Solomon from his course of self-gratification and inordinate lust. He warned him, rebuked him, and allowed three adversaries to oppose him. God told Solomon he was going to lose the kingdom and that Israel was going to be disgraced and rejected because of his action. Surely the wisest man who ever lived could not plead that he was unaware of what would transpire.

Solomon stands as an illustration of what happens when lust controls an individual. It radically distorts his judgment and his perspective. Put another way, the person's whole being is inverted so that the visceral dominates the cerebral. The prophet Nehemiah thought it best to remind Israel, "Was it not because of marriages like these that Solomon king of Israel sinned? ... even he was led into sin by foreign women" (13:26).

For Christian leaders the point is clear. One way Satan will try to destroy the leader's testimony—and that of those associated with him—is through illicit sex. *Christianity Today* recently reported that one out of ten ministers has had affairs with members of their congregations. The leader must not start down the path of immorality in his mind through sexual fantasies induced by magazines, photographs, movies, or conversation. All such must be decisively set aside so that the leader does not capitulate in his thought life. If he fails there, he will capitulate in his behavior also.

Sometimes people accept the fallacy that it is only the socially deprived or the ignorant who are sexually promiscuous. That is not true. Like Solomon, unfortunately, the highly educated and the ones who clearly know the consequences go down the same sordid road.

Wisdom, understanding, and perception are not in and of themselves sufficient to keep an individual from deliberately disobeying the explicit commands in God's Holy Word. I do not speak about those obscure passages where God's people down through the centuries have differed but of those unambiguous commandments and absolutes about which there is no debate from anyone who accepts the reliability and creditability of Holy Scripture.

Wisdom More Comprehensive Now

Wisdom is not enough. But at the same time, for those of us who are in Christ wisdom has a much more comprehensive connotation than Solomon could possibly understand.

> It is because of him that you are in Christ Jesus, who has become for us wisdom from God—that is, our righteousness, holiness and redemption. (1 Corinthians 1:30)

This distinction is important. Solomon had extraordinary wisdom in knowing the right decisions to make. He possessed unusual mental ability. But New Testament wisdom—wisdom in Christ Jesus—is more than that. This wisdom, supernaturally mediated to us in our Savior, gives us not only sensitivity but also the ability to live lives of righteousness and holiness and redemption. This is truly *liberating* wisdom.

In 1 Corinthians 2 Paul goes on to use his own life to illustrate the concept he had just introduced. Probably Paul can be singled out as the most brilliant and intelligent man mentioned in the New Testament. Besides being naturally gifted, Paul had an excellent education. His self-appraisal, then, is significant.

> When I came to you, brothers, I did not come with eloquence or superior wisdom as I proclaimed to you the testimony about God. For I resolved to know nothing while I was with you except Jesus Christ and him crucified. I came to you in weakness and fear, and with much trembling. My message and my preaching were not with wise and persuasive words, but with a demonstration of the Spirit's power, so that your faith might not rest on men's wisdom, but on God's power. (vv. 1-5)

Years ago in New England we heard about a young woman who said she was no longer a Christian. She had made a profession of faith under the ministry of one of the most brilliant men I have ever known, a man who had not only an outstanding mind but also a singular dedication to scholarship. As she listened to him, the young woman was impressed with the logic and comprehensiveness of his presentation.

Then the minister was called of God to another part of the country. When he left, the young woman's faith collapsed. She was a professing Christian only so long as her teacher was there. Once he was gone, she lost her interest in Christianity.

The Apostle Paul knew of that possibility. So do most preachers. One of the greatest temptations they have is to minister in the energy of the flesh. When I was a student at the University of Chicago, I took a course in American religious movements. The professor told of clinical studies of meetings in which the evangelist had everything carefully orchestrated. At the end of each sermon was a deathbed tale or other tear-jerking story. Then, as soft music played in the background, people were influenced by an emotional appeal by the preacher to come down to the front. Whether or not the gospel was being presented seemed immaterial. Through mass psychology people would come forward in any case.

Admittedly, such manipulation is possible. But the results that endure come when our witness is characterized by the wisdom God has given us, so that it is not our cleverness but the Lord who is glorified. Then people will respond genuinely and lastingly—because of the authenticity of what we had to say about Jesus Christ.

The great evangelist D. L. Moody was accused of murdering the King's English. The fact that he may have done so does not justify the practice, but his ministry illustrates for us the distinction between an eloquent, finely honed sermon that is devoid of spiritual power and one characterized by the dynamic of the Holy Spirit. The one celebrates man's wisdom; the other elevates God's power.

Righteousness, holiness, and redemption—these were Paul's themes. The contrast between the wisdom of Solomon and that of Paul may be seen not only in his personal example but in the Biblical and historical examples of churches and other Christian institutions.

One of the most striking of these was the church at Laodicea, described in Revelation 3. This congregation's self-perception was highly favorable, but the criterion is of utmost significance: it was material well-being. "You say, 'I am rich; I have acquired wealth and do not need a thing'" (v. 17). This one-dimensional assessment failed to recognize the spiritual bankruptcy so graphically portrayed in the text ("wretched, pitiful, poor, blind and naked").

Examples could be multiplied from church history—even to the present time—when endowments, buildings, membership lists, and multiple staffs are perceived as signs of success.

Nowhere is the reliance on material well-being more evident than in the history of Christian higher education. As many institutions became more prestigious and more heavily endowed, they lost their spiritual vibrancy and eventually their Christian characteristics. We may ask why these things came to pass. I believe the change began with the leadership.

Similarly, as was true at Yale during Timothy Dwight's presidency, this tendency can be reversed. As Solomon started Israel toward eventual apostasy, so the Apostle Paul summoned the early church to orthodoxy.

Our own times cry out for informed, resolute leadership with a clear-eyed vision of Biblical ideals that will rally churches, Christian colleges, and other Christian organizations to look beyond human wisdom to divine revelation. Then the inversion of values will be stopped, and spiritual formation will proceed to the glory of God and the edification of His people.

15

Consistent Growth

The Apostle Peter's motto as he confronted each new challenge might well have been, "Take action!" As a result his mistakes tended to be public and dramatic, but the saving feature of his career was his continuing desire to improve. Analyzing Peter's progress toward maturity will aid the leader of today in his own growth. Far from thinking he has attained (cf. Philippians 3:12), the effective leader should continually seek to learn from his experiences and become even more proficient in his work.

Growth Is Often Painful

As I have observed, one of Peter's major problems was his tendency to act first and think later. For example:

> During the fourth watch of the night Jesus went out to them, walking on the lake. . . . "Lord, if it's you . . . tell me to come to you on the water." "Come," he said. Then Peter got down out of the boat and walked on the water to Jesus. But when he saw the wind, he was afraid and, beginning to sink, cried out, "Lord, save me!" Immediately Jesus reached out his hand and caught him. (Matthew 14:25-31)

This experience typified Peter's manner of life, and it highlighted his need to mature. Over and over Peter responded in immediate but unthinking enthusiasm to the challenge of the moment and then had second thoughts as the realities of the situation became clear to him. Fortunately, by one means or another he was again and again corrected and restored. Gradually he had an awareness of what it meant to serve the Lord, but this attitude resulted only after some painful experiences. One of these was when Peter acknowledged Jesus as the Son of the living God and then immediately challenged Christ's statement about His going to the cross.

> Jesus . . . asked his disciples, "Who do people say the Son of Man is?" . . . Simon Peter answered, "You are the Christ, the Son of the living God." Jesus replied, "Blessed are you, Simon son of Jonah, for this was not revealed to you by man, but by my Father in heaven." . . . From that time on Jesus began to explain to his disciples that . . . he must be killed and on the third day be raised to life. . . . Peter began to rebuke him. "Never, Lord!" he said. "This shall never happen to you!" (Matthew 16:13-22)

When the Lord told Peter it was not flesh and blood but the Father in Heaven who revealed the person of Christ to him, He was saying that such an insight came only through revelation from God. This made Peter's subsequent rebuke of the Lord the more serious.

While he was divinely ordained to receive special revelation and to articulate it, and did this with enthusiasm, Peter apparently did not comprehend what his confession meant. Otherwise, how could he by divine revelation confess Jesus as the Messiah, Son of the living God, and so soon afterward rebuke Him for saying He was meant to suffer and die?

Pride Is a Constant Pitfall

Perhaps, in addition to acting impulsively, Peter contradicted our Lord because he had become proud about being the recipient of divine revelation. Having had this disclosure from God, he may have thought he was now competent to render a judgment on any subject whatsoever.

I have found some Christians to be that way. Because they have a comprehensive knowledge of one field and have become expert in it, they conclude they are authorities about almost everything else as well. Unfortunately, such expertise does not necessarily follow. Nor does one experience indicate that all succeeding experiences are going to be the same. Knowledge does not beget knowledge or victory victory. A degree of humility would spare such individuals the dire results of such presumption.

Those in higher education face this issue constantly. Having had unusual opportunities to become knowledgeable, some find it easy to elevate this expertise to an unwarranted absoluteness. Just because someone with a Ph.D. says something does not necessarily make it so. How tragic to see an educated person unwilling to apply the same rigorous investigative and evaluative procedures to other fields of knowledge that he brings to his own discipline!

When I was a historian, I was meticulous in looking up the sources and in having two or three references for every fact I cited. Yet I found it easy to accept a rumor without testing its validity. In such matters I was not employing the rigorous tests for truth that were standard procedure in my discipline. Similarly, Peter should have concluded that since he was the recipient of divine revelation, he was obliged to take this into account in his assessment of Jesus' statements.

Self-preservation Distorts Perspective

Some earnest but misguided Christians have concluded that some of the Biblical writers were wrong. I am disturbed when I hear such talk, and I think of the Lord's rebuke to Peter (Matthew 16:23). Distrust of God's Word does the work of the enemy. Remember, the first time God's Word was questioned was in the Garden of Eden, when Satan remarked, "Did God really say?" (Genesis 3:1). That same question regarding the Word of God is present with us today.

So when Jesus retorted to Peter, "Out of my sight, Satan! You are a stumbling block to me; you do not have in mind the things of God, but the things of men," He knew very well that the campaign that was begun in the Garden of Eden was being continued through the one who had just been commended as a vehicle of divine revelation.

This incident should give us pause because it suggests that those of us who know the Lord and who are His disciples might be tempted in the same way. We need to be extraordinarily careful as we come to God's Word that we do not question its truthfulness, for that opens the way for the enemy to come in and exploit the situation for his own ends.

The question remains, however, as to whether anything else motivated Peter to challenge the Lord. I believe that the same concern for self-preservation Peter exhibited on other occasions (for instance, in Matthew 14:30) may have been present here. Notice that immediately after our Savior rebuked Peter, Jesus outlined the conditions to be met by those desiring to be His disciples:

"If anyone would come after me, he must deny himself and take up his cross and follow me. For whoever wants to save his life will lose it, but whoever loses his life for me will find it. What good will it be for a man if he gains the whole world, yet forfeits his soul?" (Matthew 16:24-26)

I am convinced that when the Apostle Peter heard Jesus declare that He was going to go to Jerusalem where He would suffer many things from the elders and chief priests and scribes and in fact be killed, Peter became so agitated by the possible threat to him personally that he did not hear the Lord also say He would be raised the third day.

Some may wonder whether such selective deafness is really possible. I assure you that it is, for I have behaved in much the same way. I have been listening to a sermon when I would begin to muse about what the minister had just been discussing. He, meanwhile, would continue his preaching. Soon I would ruefully discover that I had missed an entire intervening sequence because of my preoccupation with what had been said earlier. I had not been listening.

Similarly, I believe Peter's attention span had been broken before the Lord was speaking about being raised the third day. Preoccupied with saving his own skin, Peter rebuked the Lord in an effort to change His mind. Jesus' response is instructive. After rebuking Peter to emphasize His Lordship, He then encouraged Peter and the other disciples to focus on their ultimate goals and destiny (vv. 24-28).

In many ways this experience in Peter's life parallels the time he walked on the water. At that time, as he looked at the circumstances all his confidence in the Lord and His power was displaced by anxiety for his own safety. As a result he began to sink, and Peter needed to be rescued by the Lord. Now Peter began to sink into unbelief because of a concern for his own welfare. He required the Savior's strong and realistic intervention to overcome his doubts and restore his faith.

To all who acknowledge their commitment as disciples of Jesus Christ, this message is timeless. It may be natural to feel threatened when facing the prospect of tribulation and persecution. But for Jesus' disciples escape must not be an option. Instead, there must be a resolute decision to follow Christ at all costs, recognizing that the eternal rewards are both glorious and enduring.

The Lessons Continue

Another instance of Peter's propensity toward hasty response followed by chagrin is detailed in the familiar story found in Matthew 26.

Then Jesus told them, "This very night you will all fall away on account of me." . . . Peter replied, "Even if all fall away on account of you, I never will." "I tell you the truth," Jesus answered, "this very night, before the rooster crows, you will disown me three times." But Peter declared, "Even if I have to die with you, I will never disown you." (vv. 31-35)

Here again the pattern is evident in Peter's enthusiastic pledge of allegiance. This time, however, the Lord spoke directly to Peter before he was confronted with the circumstance. The Lord understood Peter's tendency and knew that when he got into a threatening circumstance, he would deny his Master. It was almost as if Jesus was asking Peter to remember what had happened to him before. He clearly pointed out Peter's problem.

Despite the Lord's divine insight, Peter was not ready to accept the possibility of his denying Jesus. His attitude seemed to be that though he may have failed his Lord in the past, now he had enough self-confidence and trust in his convictions never to deny Him again. The Apostle Paul's later words in 1 Corinthians 10:12 are relevant here—"if you think you are standing firm, be careful that you don't fall!"

See how patient the Lord is with His disciple. When Peter walked on the water and then began to sink, the Savior reminded him that he had but little faith. Peter should have had more faith in Christ and less concern for circumstances. Then when Peter had the divine revelation about Christ's person, the Lord had to remind him that this truth, rather than his own well-being, must be central. Now Jesus once again urges Peter to recognize that his natural tendency will be to flee because of threatening circumstances. Yet Peter still was not able to confront his problem. Again he was presumptuous, rejecting the Lord's forewarning.

The fulfillment of this prediction is described in the closing part of chapter 26 of Matthew (vv. 69-75), where Peter's repeated denials are described. This sequence, I believe, marks a turning point in the growth of this man. He encountered a crisis that others also have experienced in their Christian walk. When we trust in ourselves apart from God's grace and power, there will be occasions when we will realize with painful awareness the complete poverty of our own resources to cope with the particular issue that has come into our lives. In Peter's case it was a misplaced self-confidence that got him into the crisis in which he acted to protect himself despite the commitments he had made. All of this combined to show him just how needy he was.

For years I was troubled when I read that Peter denied Jesus with an oath and began to curse and swear, for I projected a twentieth-century concept of cursing and swearing into the situation. Now I think that what Peter did was to use the oaths that for a Jew were binding. However, that makes his actions even more pathetic. In our parlance he was standing up, putting one hand on the Bible, and raising the other hand to say, "I solemnly swear to tell the truth, the whole truth, and nothing but the truth, so help me, God—I do not know that man."

When the cock crowed and Peter remembered Jesus' words, the realization of what he had done struck him with great force. No doubt he recalled that he had not only declared his intentions privately in the presence of the disciples, but also had publicly affirmed, as if he were an honorable man whose word was to be trusted, that he did not even know his Lord. He had completely contradicted what he had told Jesus earlier. Thus God graciously permitted Peter to be brought to the point where with great clarity he could see what his problem really was.

A Blessed Restoration

Thank God, the Lord did not simply leave Peter in a state of painful awareness. Rather, He provided an opportunity for Peter's restoration to fellowship and meaningful service once Peter was prepared to grow in his faith and to seek to apply it in practice. The method the Savior used to renew Peter's commitment is described in the well-known passage in John 21 where three times the Savior pressed the point as to whether Peter really loved Him. Now notice what immediately follows:

> "I tell you the truth, when you were younger you dressed yourself and went where you wanted; but when you are old you will stretch out your hands, and someone else will dress you and lead you where you do not want to go." Jesus said this to indicate the kind of death by which Peter would glorify God. Then he said to him, "Follow me!" (vv. 18, 19)

In this way the Lord spoke directly to the major issue in Peter's life. He had permitted Peter to get himself into a circumstance in which he denied the Lord three times. Then He graciously questioned Peter to give him an opportunity for realistic but heartfelt reaffirmation of his commitment. But with the commissioning to feed the lambs and tend the sheep, the Lord immediately brought up the issue of self-preservation. He told Peter that his concern about jeopardy in serving Christ was actually well-founded. When he became older, Peter would indeed die a martyr's death. And yet in light of that prospect, because Peter had just told the Lord that he loved Him, he was issued the command, "Follow me."

There is beautiful drama here. Memories from Peter's past experiences must have crowded in upon him. He probably recalled walking on the water and then being afraid for his own safety because he was not looking at the Lord but at the circumstances. He remembered hearing Jesus affirm He was going to be crucified and how he feared for his own life. He called to mind the Lord's statement that the disciples—including himself—would be scattered. He thought about his objection to that prediction and his subsequent three-fold denial.

As all this swept before him, Peter was now ready to assess himself realistically. No doubt he remembered the Lord's word, recorded in Matthew 16:24, that to be a disciple he would have to deny himself and take up his cross. Before Peter really understood the crucifixion, that might well have been an abstract thought; now it was a reality. From afar Peter could see his Savior stretched out upon the cross. He could hear the curses of the crowd and their mocking and jeering. In his mind's eye he could see blood dripping from the Savior's body. Surely these vivid impressions were his when the Lord told Peter others would take him where he did not want to go, signifying the kind of death he was to die.

Tradition says Peter was crucified upside-down at his own request because he did not want to be executed in the same posture as his Savior. If this is true, it suggests that Peter not only realistically faced the fact that to serve Jesus Christ and to follow Him would involve the losing of his life in a brutal and cruel way, but also suggests that even in this experience he wanted to convey his subordination to His sovereign Lord.

Let us be forewarned and humbled to know that the Lord will test us at the point of our vulnerability, at that point most calculated to interfere with our devotion to Him. For Peter it was physical self-preservation. For the rich young ruler it was his possessions. For some of us it might be our reputation, our family, our health, or our special capabilities. Whatever it is, the Lord will challenge us at the very point where this particular factor will interfere with our unconditional commitment to Him. We should also avoid the temptation of thinking that whatever testing we may experience should be the lot of other Christians as well, or that somehow we are deprived if the Lord apparently tests us more severely than some of His other disciples.

Fellow Believers Aid Growth

Such testing that does come our way, however, does not necessarily guarantee we will consistently apply our commitment to circumstances or events now or in the future. To insure consistency and growth requires the ongoing ministry of the Lord in our lives. Frequently this is mediated to us through fellow members of the Body of Christ.

The second chapter of Galatians includes the account of how one of Peter's brothers in the faith (the Apostle Paul) assumed the role Jesus had filled in dealing with Peter during His incarnate ministry. Paul notes:

> When Peter came to Antioch, I opposed him to his face, because he was in the wrong. Before certain men came from James, he used to eat with the Gentiles. But when they arrived, he began to draw back and separate himself from the Gentiles because he was afraid of those who belonged to the circumcision group. The other Jews joined him in his hypocrisy, so that by their hypocrisy even Barnabas was led astray. When I saw that they were not acting in line with the truth of the gospel, I said to Peter in front of them all, "You are a Jew, yet you live like a Gentile and not like a Jew. How is it, then, that you force Gentiles to follow Jewish customs?" (vv. 11-14)

In the remainder of the chapter Paul summarizes his conversation with Peter.

The fact that Paul's rebuke was necessary was all the more remarkable because of what had happened to Peter as described in Acts 10. In preparation for the message from Cornelius, who was a Gentile, God allowed Peter to see a vision of a sheet let down from Heaven with all kinds of creatures on it. Peter was hungry and heard a voice telling him to kill these and eat them. Interestingly, Peter's familiar tendency to question the Lord showed itself even then. "'Surely not, Lord!' Peter replied. 'I have never eaten anything impure or unclean'" (v. 14). To this protest the voice replied that what God had cleansed, Peter was not to call unclean. For emphasis the experience was repeated three times.

I can sympathize with Peter because in my own experience I have had difficulty on occasion putting a propositional truth into action. In the late 1960s we saw changes on the Wheaton College campus, not only in attitude but also in the appearance of some of our students. I then held (and still hold) some convictions about men having long hair. I believe it is inappropriate and Biblically unjustified. Our student personnel staff urged, however, that we permit a degree of liberty in this matter.

We had some young men on campus whose hair was longer than I thought it should have been. They also began to dress in a manner more like the counterculture, which I deplored because to me the counterculture represented unpatriotic draft-resisters, flag-burners, and such like. When I read of their acts as they rioted and demonstrated, my blood pressure rose because I remembered fighting for the country they seemed to despise. Though I had fought for all citizens to have the liberty to disagree, I resented the way the counterculture went about disagreeing.

One day I was scheduled to speak in chapel. Just before the service, we gathered for prayer to ask the Lord's blessing. As we were about to pray, in walked a young man who had a beard and long hair, was wearing a sash around his waist, and had on sandals. As I looked at him, I was sorry he had come. Worse yet, he sat down right beside me.

When we went to prayer, I did not enter into the praying with a very good attitude. Then the young man began to pray, and his prayer went something like this: "Dear Lord, you know how much I admire Dr. Armerding, how I appreciate his walk with You. I am grateful for what a man of God he is, and how he loves You and loves Your people. Lord, bless him today. Give him liberty in the Holy Spirit, and make him a real blessing to all of us in the student body. Help us to have open hearts to hear what he has to say, and may we just do what You want us to do."

As I walked down the steps to go into the chapel, the Lord spoke to me about my attitude. After giving my message, I asked the young man to come to the platform. Later I learned that one of the students turned to another at that point and remarked that I was probably about to dismiss the young man from school as an example to the rest of the students. Thus everyone, including the young man, was surprised when I put my arms around him and embraced him as a brother in Christ. That dramatically ended the chapel service. Students stood and applauded; they cried and embraced each other. The situation was unprecedented and, under God, seemed to change the mood on campus to one of greater love and acceptance of one another.

I was informed later that the young man in question had adopted his appearance in order to be able to reach some of his generation who were alienated. Whether or not this was the case, I needed to learn not to reject someone whom God had cleansed. If God has accepted another believer, I should do so as well. I should not reject him simply because of his style of life.

Fortunately, Peter was open to the Lord's instruction given him in the vision, even though it meant readjusting his manner of life after years of doing things a certain way. Thus he responded positively when he was invited to the household of Cornelius and was candid enough to share his experience with them. Then he saw the Lord work in a supernatural way, confirming the leading he had been given, as the Holy Spirit came upon the Gentiles.

But later, in spite of this meaningful experience which was endorsed by the church leaders in Jerusalem, a problem began to arise in Peter's mind. He reflected upon the fact that his status with his Jewish brethren might be jeopardized by his associating with Christians who were Gentiles. So once again the expediency of the moment prompted him to withdraw from having fellowship with the Gentiles so as not to offend his Jewish brethren.

In confronting Peter, the Apostle Paul was God's instrument to remind him of what he knew very well but was not practicing. So Paul faced him with the fact that he, being a Jew, was living like the Gentiles. Hence it was not right for Peter to expect the Gentile believers to live as the Jewish Christians were persuaded they should. In saying this, Paul was summoning Peter to live out what he knew by putting aside his anxieties about his status with his Jewish brethren and by accepting in practice the unity of the Body of Christ.

Here again the Apostle Peter needed to grow. While he was no longer questioning whether his life was to be taken, he still had a problem about his relationship with others. Resolving this situation was a major advance in his growth in grace.

Application for Us

These incidents in Peter's experience correspond to the three major foes we must face. In Matthew 16:13-23 Peter's enemy was Satan. In Matthew 26:69-75 his enemy was his concern for his flesh. In Galatians 2:1-14 his enemy was his reputation with his world, the world of Jewish culture. The world, the flesh, and the Devil still work together today to stunt the spiritual growth of the Christian leader and to reduce his commitment to the Lordship of Jesus Christ.

Specific evidence for Peter's spiritual growth may be found in his first epistle. The passages I shall mention are only representative. A careful reading of 1 and 2 Peter will make plain that both of these epistles contain numerous references to the very matters we have been discussing.

In 1 Peter 5:8, 9 I believe the apostle refers to the experience recorded in Matthew 16:

Be self-controlled and alert. Your enemy the devil prowls around like a roaring lion looking for someone to devour. Resist him, standing firm in the faith, because you know that your brothers throughout the world are undergoing the same kind of sufferings.

Peter had learned that Satan was a formidable foe but one who could be successfully resisted through Christ.

Then in chapter 2 of this same epistle, verses 11 and 12 tell us:

Dear friends, I urge you, as aliens and strangers in the world, to abstain from sinful desires, which war against your soul. Live such good lives among the pagans that, though they accuse you of doing wrong, they may see your good deeds and glorify God on the day he visits us.

From this statement we know that Peter had learned not to give way to the flesh, even for self-preservation, that he might be a good witness for his Savior.

Consider also his statement in 1 Peter 3:

Who is going to harm you if you are eager to do good? But even if you should suffer for what is right, you are blessed. "Do not fear what they fear; do not be frightened." But in your hearts set apart Christ as Lord. Always be prepared to give an answer to everyone who asks you to give the reason for the hope that you have. But do this with gentleness and respect, keeping a clear conscience, so that those who speak maliciously against your good behavior in Christ may be ashamed of their slander. It is better, if it is God's will, to suffer for doing good than for doing evil. (vv. 13-17)

Peter had grasped that faithfulness to the will of God was paramount, whether or not this was acceptable to those around him.

In the closing years of his life, therefore, Peter had come to some settled convictions. He would not allow Satan to take advantage of him but would resist him, being steadfast in the faith. He would not permit his fleshly desires to get out of hand and cause his testimony to be compromised, but would keep his body disciplined under the sovereign power of the Holy Spirit. He would not have his behavior influenced by others, but would take his stand and be willing to suffer for Jesus' sake. To me, these are clear indications of spiritual growth.

The Christian leader should carefully examine himself to identify those characteristics in his life that may be interfering with an uncompromising devotion to the Lord Jesus Christ. Then he should be ready to learn from the circumstances through which the Lord might put him. Thereafter he should continue to grow in perception and in understanding so that as he comes to the close of life he may be able out of the richness and fullness of experience and conviction to say to others as Peter did in the last verse of his second epistle, "Grow in the grace and knowledge of our Lord and Savior Jesus Christ. . . ."

16

Leadership's Final Challenge

O f all of the challenges the Christian leader encounters, perhaps none is more daunting than the renunciation, voluntary or otherwise, of the leadership role as one grows old in
years. This is accompanied by the realization, painful at times, that
growing older imposes limitations which are primarily physical but
may also include the mental and the emotional. "Grow old along
with me/The best is yet to be" is a gallant romanticism that may be a
distinct possibility but not an assured idyll. And usually the passage
of the years needs to be faced far more realistically than is generally
the case.

Youth Culture Glorified

Our culture has largely inverted the Biblical status accorded to the
elderly. Not-too-successful or even pathetic efforts are made to retain
a youthful appearance because it is well understood that our society
celebrates this. The result is a substantial, and seldom justified, investment in cosmetics, surgical procedures, and artificial adornments
which are marshaled to delay or mask the certainty of "to dust you
will return" (Genesis 3:19).

Such endeavors are innocent enough, I suppose, despite inordinate preoccupation with them which can interfere with "seeing life
steadily and seeing it whole," as Matthew Arnold put it. But far more

sinister is a growing attitude in our time that views older people with resentment and hostility. Due to improved medical procedures, better diet, and more sensible attitudes toward indulgence and exercise, it is anticipated that by the year 2035 the over-sixty-five segment of our population will have doubled. With the resulting need for increasingly expensive health care and the substantial acceleration of Social Security payments, coupled with the notion that the elderly are unproductive and thus parasitic, the oncoming generation shows signs of moving toward an adversarial position.

Irritation in some instances displaces respect for the aged. A prominent political figure was even quoted as advising older people to die and get out of the way—a behavior pattern predicted years ago by Huxley in *Brave New World* and apparently advocated by the Hemlock Society.

When to Step Down

Thus the confluence of personal frustration and nascent social antipathy furnish the mature but aging Christian leader with a formidable challenge. On the one hand, encouragement to continue can be derived from seeing some of the political leaders of the world functioning in their seventies and eighties. Then, too, anti-discrimination legislation has been passed that has largely invalidated the proposition attributed to Bismarck that sixty-five is the normal retirement age. On the other hand, motivation to retire is prompted by the need to effect an orderly transfer of responsibility and to make room for qualified subordinates to assume executive prerogatives.

The realism of declining competence, too often recognized by others long before the leader perceives what is happening, is a contributing factor as well. Fortunate indeed is the leader who identifies this phenomenon before it brings about a caricature of a once dynamic performance. And fortunate also is the organization whose leader, at the right time, actually and not just symbolically steps aside.

I recall a Christian leader, whose retirement had been announced, commenting that he welcomed his successor's arrival to help him continue to run the organization. Understandably, the successor refused to come until it was clear that he and not his predecessor would be in charge. In my own case, when I left the office of president of Wheaton College I stayed away from the campus for three months to avoid any inadvertent reentry into the province of authority now administered by my successor.

One Christian leader who had recently retired said that his reactions to leaving office seemed to follow the sequence of feelings we have after a bereavement: grief, loss, denial, questioning, and finally acceptance. For him these reactions were accentuated as he watched his successor receive the attention and loyalty that had been his. I suggest that the longer we are in office, the more probable these reactions will be. Fortunately, in this case the sequence of feelings ended with a sense of freedom and peace.

Scripture Provides Direction

Granted that cultural mores and personal feelings are powerful and pervasive, the Christian community must find its direction from Biblical rather than societal norms and thus be true to the finest elements of its heritage.

Basic to a realistic perspective is the brevity and uncertainty of life. Most human beings, and indeed most Christians, give only spasmodic and perfunctory attention to this reality. Even for the elderly, death is viewed as an unwelcome and unexpected happening. In the absence of a dreadful terminal illness, the expectation prevails that the plans for the future will work out. A relatively small number of reasonably healthy and lucid older people would state what Malcolm Muggeridge told me during his last visit to Wheaton: "I am going home to learn how to die." Yet Scripture would seem to recommend this attitude not only to the aged but to *all* the believing community.

Our Lord called a certain man a fool for presuming he would live for many years (Luke 12:16-21). In a similar vein, the epistle of James

(4:13-15) reminds us that we really do not know what will happen tomorrow, let alone a year or more in the future. The imagery is vivid: a mist that appears for a little while and then vanishes. To be sure, God did tell Hezekiah he would live an additional fifteen years (2 Kings 20:1-6), and God revealed to Simeon (Luke 2:25, 26) that he would not die until he had seen the Lord's Christ. But these are exceptional instances. The uncertainty of the duration of our earthly pilgrimage and the certainty of the fulfillment of God's judgment on the human race (death, Hebrews 9:27) must be recognized by the Christian leader.

We should accept the fact also that each day is a gift from God to be used to glorify Him (Psalm 118:24). This can be liberating as we recognize the fresh opportunities before us and perceive also that God, in giving us the day, must have a purpose for us in it. The challenge is to seize the opportunities and then trust the Lord for enablement (see, for example, Colossians 4:2-6). I suggest this permits the leader to be realistic without being morbid and to rest in the assurance that indeed he is immortal, as the saying goes, until his work is done.

God Numbers Our Days

Not only those who have been in combat, but also those who perceptively view what happens to people in general recognize that there is no satisfactory rationale, humanly speaking, as to why some are saved from death and others are not. But the Christian does have the substantial comfort that comes from knowing that our times are in God's hands. The translator and writer J. B. Phillips has put it this way: "In Christ . . . death can be safely ignored and Heaven confidently welcomed." Having this assurance does not necessarily eliminate the sudden bewilderment of an unexpected bereavement, but it does in time become the stabilizing force that saves us from prolonged despair or, worse, an excess of profligacy: eat, drink and be merry, for tomorrow we die.

The divine dynamics that govern our length of days are perceived but dimly by us, though there are some Scriptural promises which address the issue of how long we shall be on this earth. The Fifth Commandment (Exodus 20:12), reiterated in the New Testament (Ephesians 6:2, 3), promises long life to those who honor their father and mother. Further, note the correlation between reverence for the Lord and His extension of our days (Proverbs 10:27—"The fear of the Lord adds length to life"; see also Psalm 91:16—"With long life will I satisfy him").

Naturally, for His own inscrutable purposes, our sovereign Lord may shorten a life we have every expectation should be long, but even this may be a merciful intervention to shield the individual Christian from indulging latent disobedience (consider King Hezekiah, mentioned in an earlier chapter) or from experiencing destructive tribulation. What helps me is to recognize that our God is loving and purposeful, not capricious and sadistic.

In any case, we should be worshipful and obedient with the expectation that for us the Scriptural promises will find fulfillment—and if not, that there was a perfectly good reason it was not to be.

Approaches to Later Years

Granted the inexorable progression of the years and, for some leaders at least, the reality of resignation or retirement, induced or freely chosen as an option, what should be done afterward with one's time? Some will pursue amusement with something of the same diligence they displayed in the executive suite—a quest, in my judgment, that can result in superficiality and the atrophy of perfectly good capabilities. Of course, this imbalance may prevail before as well as after retirement. Preoccupation with furnishings, automobiles, memberships, and such like results in a needless and sometimes hurtful diversion from assigned tasks. Similarly, the perquisites of office can command attention to such an extent that there is a neglect of vigorous stewardship of executive responsibility.

Or, since things seem to be going well, the temptation may be to coast—"drift" might be a better word—into the Kingdom. This can be a perilous position to be in, for our vulnerabilities can easily be exploited, casting a shadow over an otherwise distinguished career.

I believe this was true of Solomon, who provides a case study of how inordinate and unrestrained sexual passion can produce a distortion of judgment that could rightly be defined as a kind of insanity. Surely God wanted his fall to be recorded for the instruction and warning of others after Solomon who would also have high privilege and prerogative.

The dismal incidents from the world of contemporary Christian leadership only underscore how seriously the Scriptural warnings should be heeded. Perhaps more than others, Christian leaders live in an atmosphere of vulnerability, and growing older does not necessarily deliver us from it. Indeed, a more relaxed pace may permit mental discipline to be less rigorous and thus leave one vulnerable to seductive imaginations. Unchecked, these can come to dominate both thinking and emotion.

With the maintenance of rigorous mental and circumstantial discipline, however, senior leadership that is no longer encumbered with major executive responsibility has, from the Bible itself, some notable precedents to follow. Unique to such leaders is a perspective of breadth and depth that is developed only after years of experience. In the areas of the theological, ecclesiastical, and social, Carl Henry manifests such insight, as did the late Frank Gaebelein in the area of the arts. This perspective is needed by the oncoming leadership so they will not be condemned to learn some things only by bitter and costly personal experience.

Remember, circumstances change, but human proclivities are remarkably constant. After all, interpersonal relationships and group dynamics will inevitably produce a substantial number of major challenges that are familiar issues to the leaders of the past. Those who follow in their footsteps should be aware of this.

The final statements of Moses and Joshua to the people of God in the Old Testament and the forceful and eloquent exhortations of the apostles to those in New Testament times provide models of substance for the retired leader. Too often younger leaders may fall prey to the delusion that the issues and problems they face are unique in human history. Often this fiction intrudes itself into our thinking at a low point in our experience—the mistaken notion that no one else has had to deal with quite the severity and complexity of the problem we are encountering.

For me, it has been restorative to reflect upon the Biblical accounts and to welcome the seasoned wisdom of those contemporaries who went down the road before me. We owe it to those who follow us to provide the same kind of reassurance and insight that steadied us in similar circumstances. Helpful, too, is the constant reminder drawn from Scripture that we should not think of ourselves more highly than we ought to think (Romans 12:3). We are, after all, only a microcosm in God's grand scheme of things.

Living Our Affirmations

But older leaders can make an even more personal and dynamic contribution. It is one thing to warn, exhort, and at times applaud, but quite another to *incarnate* what we affirm. Scripture commends the ministry of example as a meaningful demonstration and as an encouragement that the theoretical can indeed become the possible. We have all been amused by the detailed advice some unmarried people share freely about how to raise children. By contrast we are deeply impressed by parents whose children rise up and call them blessed— and imitate them. So it should be with leadership.

Perhaps the most notable Biblical illustration of leadership by example was the Apostle Paul. Because of his long experience of walking with the Lord, he could invite those to whom he ministered, including younger leaders, to be followers of him. Consider his testimony in such key passages as 2 Corinthians 12:1-10 or Philippians

4:10-13, where he witnessed to the balanced acceptance God developed in him through circumstances, including suffering. I concur that inviting others to follow us is a daunting prospect, but we should celebrate God's enablement in our lives, giving Him the glory, particularly in those areas where we naturally seem to have major limitations. Of all people we are the most aware of the fact that whatever was accomplished there was not because of us. But we are also the most conscious of how remarkably the power of God can work in and through a fallible believer.

It is imperative that the next generation see the evidence of God's enablement in us, for they face incredible opposition in today's world. In my career I did not have to battle those militantly organized to promote what is euphemistically (and I believe wrongly) described as an "alternate lifestyle." To call such behavior sinful today is to invite the most vicious abuse—verbal and physical, as some prominent church leaders of principle have found out in a nation formally committed to the free exercise of religion. Thus, while the challenges may be more intense and more formidable, standing for truth and righteousness is timeless in its pertinence and in its demonstration.

A Life in Perspective

A word of caution needs to be entered here. Care should be taken to avoid giving the impression that everything we did was "just right." An honest admission of mistakes and failures is not only admirable but encouraging to some whose limitations and errors loom large in their thinking.

We should also recognize that changing circumstances may warrant a different approach or methodology, without any thought of compromising immutable principles. What may have been a resounding success in one setting may simply not work in another. We should recall how we took a different approach from that of our predecessors and therefore accept this flexibility in the methods of those who succeed us. But we should demonstrate unequivocally our commitment to the authority of Scripture and neither attempt nor encourage any alteration of its absolutes.

Nor should we, deliberately or inadvertently, cause a younger leader to become dependent on us. I have seen instances of this situation where, either because of fear or insecurity, the younger leader kept looking to his mentor for ongoing direction. This does not preclude consultation but does call into question the understandable but mistaken sentiment that no major decision was to be made without the concurrence of the older leader.

When I was appointed acting dean at Gordon College, my predecessor stayed with me for a brief time and then told me I was on my own. This was almost overwhelming for me, but it was very wise on his part. I needed to be able to "fly" by myself rather than depend on him.

The same Scripture which instructs us to bear one another's burdens also directs us to carry our own load (Galatians 6:2, 5). Therefore, difficult as it may be, it is incumbent upon us to be able to admit that our successor may very well be doing a better job than we did. If so, there should be gratitude to God rather than remorse that our performance has been overshadowed. In the providence of God, our successor may have been given special capabilities that the ongoing situation required. To have the exercise of these gifts result in enthusiastic recognition is entirely justified. Surely that was our conviction in earlier years when we had a somewhat similar experience, even though it may now be long forgotten except by us.

Yet even this is but a partial perception. History tells us that what seemed at the time to be a rather lackluster performance, eclipsed by that of a charismatic successor, may not appear so later.

President Harry Truman is a recent example. When he left office to be succeeded by General Eisenhower, an enormously popular war hero, he was perceived by many as petty, capricious, and not really worthy of the high office of President of the United States. In the past few years, however, he has been described by many as one of our stronger Presidents. Similarly, Abraham Lincoln was ridiculed and stigmatized in a manner that appears extravagant even in our censorious age, but now is held in great respect by an admiring and grateful nation.

A review of our record at the point of our retirement may appear either too favorable due to the excess of emotional outpourings at the time or too defective because of the foreshortened or jaundiced perspective of the eager critics of our administration. Jeremiah, for example, may have been perceived by his contemporaries simply as a faithful but overemotional failure, but the Bible ranks him as one of the greatest of the prophets.

The evaluation of our career, moreover, has its most significant expression beyond time—in eternity. Here the sovereign Lord will render the only judgment that really counts. As we have sought to be faithful to Him, let us anticipate His "Well done." It is striking that an infinite and perfect God does not unduly magnify our failures or have these overshadow whatever we have done that brought Him glory. Instead, in grace and mercy He recognizes that which pleases Him and commends us for it.

Such an evaluation, however, will not be limited to the time we had executive responsibilities. Instead, the whole of life will be in view, including the years God may give us after we leave office. I believe He expects continued growth on our part and, because our schedules may not be so encumbered, a greater commitment to worship, praise, and intercession. This outlook can generate a heightened sense of the goodness of God and a focusing of our thanksgiving as we perceive this balance more clearly.

One of the beautiful Scriptural illustrations of the realization of God's goodness and grace is in 2 Samuel 23, which opens with this notation: "These are the last words of David." In this passage the aged monarch once again expressed his faith in the constructive purposes of God that he had come to see with increasing clarity. An exercise of this kind should be undertaken while mental powers are still functioning. In fact, it would be desirable to make a transcript of our mature and informed perspective so that family and friends will be sure to know of our profound sense of thanksgiving to our sovereign God.

Together with this awareness, however, is the cultivation of a dependence upon God for the new and sometimes virtually overwhelming experiences through which He may cause us to pass: the neglect of former associates, the awareness that we are so soon forgotten, the high probability of bereavement and loneliness, or the onset of a debilitating or terminal illness such as the cancer I have now encountered twice. In His providence God may spare us all of these, but we should seek to have that garrisoning of the soul which we may legitimately solicit from Him. It is also to be hoped that we will retain a sense of humor, for growing older can prompt laughter as well as tears.

About five years after I retired as president of Wheaton College, I returned to the campus for a visit. To memorialize its past presidents, the College has named buildings after them and by this means has kept the names of the chief executives before the succeeding generations of students. One of my predecessors, Dr. J. Oliver Buswell, Jr., served from 1926 to 1940, and the library is named after him. This gave the incident during my visit special significance.

As I was crossing the campus, a student approached me. I could tell he was studying my face intently and seemed puzzled. Then he brightened up. As we passed, he called out, "Good morning, Dr. Buswell!" *Sic transit gloria!* To this day it is a delightful and amusing recollection to which the student sincerely but unwittingly contributed.

Several years ago a dear friend and beloved colleague in Christian higher education, Dr. J. Robertson McQuilkin, composed a prayer. I shared this with the student body of Wheaton College just before I left office, and I think it fitting to include it here. I trust you will find this as meaningful as I did and as I continue to do. Perhaps the answer to this prayer will enable us to inscribe over our lives what the great composer Bach put on the music he created: *Soli Deo Gloria* (only for the glory of God).

Let Me Get Home Before Dark

    It's sundown, Lord.
The shadows of my life stretch back
    into the dimness of the years long spent.
I fear not death, for the grim foe betrays himself at last,
    thrusting me forever into life:
Life with you, unsoiled and free.

    But I do fear.
I fear that dark spectre may come too soon—
    or do I mean, too late?
That I should end before I finish or
    finish, but not well.
That I should stain your honor, shame your name,
    grieve your loving heart.
Few, they tell me, finish well . . .
Lord, let me get home before dark.

    The darkness of a spirit
    grown mean and small, fruit shriveled on the vine,
    bitter to the taste of my companions,
    burden to be borne by those brave few who love me still.
No, Lord. Let the fruit grow lush and sweet,
    A joy to all who taste;
Spirit-sign of God at work,
    stronger, fuller, brighter at the end.
Lord, let me get home before dark.

The darkness of tattered gifts,
*   rust-locked, half-spent or ill-spent,*
A life that once was used of God
*   now set aside.*
Grief for glories gone or
Fretting for a task God never gave.
Mourning in the hollow chambers of memory;
Gazing on the faded banners of victories long gone.
Cannot I run well into the end?
Lord, let me get home before dark.

The outer me decays—
*   I do not fret or ask reprieve.*
The ebbing strength but weans me from mother earth
*   and grows me up for heaven.*
I do not cling to shadows cast by immortality.
I do not patch the scaffold tent to build the real, eternal me.
I do not clutch about me my cocoon,
*   vainly struggling to hold hostage*
*   a free spirit pressing to be born.*

But will I reach the gate
*   in lingering pain, body distorted, grotesque?*
Or will it be a mind
*   wandering untethered among light phantasies or grim terrors?*
Of your grace, Father, I humbly ask . . .
Let me get home before dark.

SCRIPTURE INDEX

16:1-13	45		*Psalms*	
28:5-25	149		33:6-9	94
			66:18	149
2 Samuel			72	166
12:24	165		91:16	199
19:1-8	138		106:15	155
23	204		118:24	198
			Proverbs	
1 Kings			10:27	199
1—3	122		23:19-21	57
2:8-10	138			
6:37	169		*Isaiah*	
7:1	169		1	63
9:1-7	173		1:2-4	63
11	173		1:11-15	63
11:1-6	172		1:16, 21-23	63
11:11	173		2:2-5	63
12:7	117		25:8	47
19	134		38:2, 3	155
19:4	134		38:10-20	157
19:13	134		48:11	123
			53:6	69
2 Kings			64:6	32
16:2	152			
20:1-3	155		*Daniel*	
20:1-6	198		10:12, 13	20
20:4-6	155			
20:13-17	158		*Matthew*	
			4:17	30
1 Chronicles			5:10-12	17
28	167		5:12	23
28:9, 10	167		5:22	86
29:1	166		5:27, 28	54
29:19	166		11:29	127, 136
29:25	167		12:34, 35	87
			12:36	90
2 Chronicles			14:25-31	179
1:7	168		14:30	182
1:12	168		15:19	54
32:31	159		16	191
32:25	157		16:13-20	93
			16:13-22	180
Job			16:13-23	191
28:28	165		16:23	181
42:6	70		16:24	187
			16:24-26	182
Nehemiah			16:24-28	183
			17:1-3	137
13:26	173		19:21	72
			20:28	136
			22:35-39	65

10:12	184
10:13	24
10:31	124, 163
12	11, 44
12:7-11	108
15:58	42

2 Corinthians

1:8-11	131
2:3-11	55
10—12	131
12:1-10	201
12:9	70
12:20	87

Galatians

2	74, 188
2:1-14	191
2:11	74
2:11-14	188
3	103
3:7	104
4:4	14
5:16	54
5:19-21	54
6	47
6:1	74
6:2, 5	203
6:7, 8	47, 56

Ephesians

3:8, 9	63
3:10, 11	63
3:20	94
4:22-24	60
4:25-32	89
4:30	86
4:31	86
6:2, 3	199
6:12	20

Philippians

1:21	64
2:5-11	163
3:6	19
3:12	179
3:16	161
3:17	52
3:18, 19	51
3:19	55, 58
3:20a	51
4	131
4:10-13	163, 201

Colossians

1:18	123
4:2-6	198

1 Thessalonians

1:7	29
1:9, 10	29

2 Thessalonians

3:7-13	39
3:10-15	48

1 Timothy

3:1	123
4:12	51
4:12-16	27
5:17, 18	48
6:6-10	59
6:10	99

2 Timothy

2:10-12	50

Hebrews

4	42
4:12	88
4:16	167
5:8	69
5:8, 9	14
9:27	198
11	24, 58, 71, 92, 94, 95
11:1-6	91
11:3	94
11:4	94
11:5	95
11:8-11	96
11:11	101
11:13	71, 97
11:17	103
11:19	103
11:24	109
11:25-27	109
12:5, 6	69
12:11	69
12:15	86

James

1:5, 6	168
1:8	31
4:13-15	198

GENERAL INDEX

Aaron, 44, 113, 114, 128, 129, 130, 133
Abel, 91, 94, 95
Abner, 138
Abraham, 45, 58, 95, 96, 97, 100, 101,
   102, 103, 104, 122
   children of, 104
Absalom, 116,138
Accountability, 9, 15, 46, 47, 48, 49, 50,
   90, 119, 120, 132, 133, 134, 148, 152,
   165, 166, 171
Adam, 9
Administrative tasks, vii, 13, 115, 116, 118,
   119, 120, 132, 138
Agag the King, 147
Agape, 67 also see *Love*
Ahaz, 152
Amasa, 138
Ambition, 116, 121, 122, 123, 127, 131
   Christian, 123, 124
Amoz, 155
Ananias and Sapphira, 170
Antioch College, 149
Apollos, 45
Armerding, Carreen, 24
Armerding, Miriam, viii
Armerding, Taylor, 103
Arnold, Matthew, 195
Atheism, 92
Augustine, 16, 151

Babel, the Tower of, 85
Bach, 206
Balance, 11, 13, 40, 45, 57, 105, 109, 162,
   202, 204
Barnabas, 45, 188
Bezalel, 44, 108
Bismarck, 196
Bitterness, 86
Blessedness, blessings, 17, 18, 19, 20, 23,
   25, 43, 58, 70, 71, 90, 96, 107, 108,
   132, 136, 142, 157, 158, 161, 162, 163,
   165, 166, 167, 168, 192, 201
Bonner, William J., viii

"Boss Must Be Boss, The" (Douglas
   McGregor), 149
Brave New World (Huxley), 196
Browning, Robert, 66
Buswell, J. Oliver, Jr., 124, 205

Cain, 91
Calling, vii, 9, 10, 16, 27, 42, 43, 44, 45,
   46, 49, 51, 62, 64, 78, 109, 110, 111,
   113, 121, 123, 125, 136 see also
   Vocation
Campus Crusade, 106
China, 45, 112, 139
Christian community, the, 10, 11, 17, 25,
   39, 52, 53, 54, 64, 76, 82, 150, 197 also
   see *Faith, community of*
Christianity Today, 107, 174
Church, the, 11, 43, 63, 64, 154, 168, 170,
   176
   as a body, the Body of Christ, 11, 44,
   75, 188, 191
   church history, 64, 66, 71, 99, 153, 176
Circumstances, 45, 71, 88, 111, 121, 122,
   129, 139, 142, 143, 144, 149, 159, 171,
   183, 184, 186, 187, 193, 200, 202
Clark University, 57
Cleansing, 22, 75, 188
Columbia Bible College and Seminary, viii
Commitment to God or Christ, 16, 19, 30,
   36, 50, 61, 62, 63, 64, 76, 79, 157, 183,
   185, 186, 187, 191, 202, 204
Communication, 81, 82, 83, 85
   from God to man, 83, 93, 94
Confession, 52, 70, 71, 84, 85, 93, 180
Consecration, 52, 61, 64
Consequences, 46, 47, 49, 59, 76, 97, 99,
   102, 150, 162, 174
Contentment, 59, 163
Conversion, 30, 32, 34, 36, 51, 162
Conviction of sin, 42, 43
Cornelius, 188, 190
Correcting other believers, 73, 74, 75, 76
Covetousness, 116, 117

215